Tales from the Carolina Panthers Sideline

Scott Fowler

Sports Publishing L.L.C.
www.sportspublishingllc.com

Director of production: Susan M. Moyer
Acquisitions editor: Mike Pearson
Developmental editor: David Brauer
Project manager: Alicia Wentworth
Copy editor: Cynthia L. McNew
Photo editor: Erin Linden-Levy
Dust jacket design: Dustin Hubbart
Imaging: Dustin Hubbart
Marketing manager: Jonathan Patterson

ISBN: 1-58261-835-6

Printed in the United States of America.

Sports Publishing L.L.C.
www.sportspublishingllc.com

To my extraordinary wife, Elise, and our three wonderful, rambunctious boys—Chapel, Salem and London.

Contents

Acknowledgments

When I told my six-year-old son Chapel that I was about to spend several months writing a book about the Carolina Panthers, he quickly replied: "I already wrote a book. I did it in kindergarten. It's about groundhogs."

"How long did it take you?" I asked.

"Three days," he said.

I wasn't nearly that fast, but this book never would have gotten done at all if not for the help of many kind people.

Many folks inside the Carolina Panthers organization deserve major thanks. First of all, let me thank the players and coaches. All of the following people were a huge help in the preparation of this book by sharing their time and insight with me in extended interviews.

From the 2003 team:

Jake and Keri Delhomme and their entire extended families in Breaux Bridge and Lafayette, Louisiana, have always made me feel welcome, both by phone and in person. They have also taught me a little Cajun culture.

Steve Smith has been exhilarating to watch and is an even better interview. Mike Rucker is classy, relentless and undoubtedly the most creative non-cursing trash talker in NFL history. Kevin Donnalley was the very first person I interviewed for this book from the 2003 team and absolutely couldn't have been more helpful.

Jeff Mitchell does the best Steve Spurrier imitation you've ever heard and is a joy to talk to. Brentson Buckner is so verbose and honest that he has a future as a broadcaster if he wants it. Coach John Fox made this book possible in the first place by resurrecting the Panthers from the depths of 1-15 and has always been very generous with his time with me.

From the earlier Panther teams:

Willie (Touchdown Machine) Green has an opinion on everything—and he's almost always right. If he ever runs for political office, I sure wouldn't want to be on the other side of those debates. Mark Rodenhauser can do anything with a computer and has a great memory to boot.

Gerald Williams and Dwight Stone represent some of the best of what those 1995 and '96 teams were about—good players and great guys. Williams ended up becoming a middle-school teacher and Stone a police officer, both in Charlotte.

Bill Rosinski, the only play-by-play man the Panthers have ever had, has the deep voice and the even deeper knowledge of this team to make it worth turning off the TV sound to listen to him. If you haven't ever done that, you need to. Jessie Armstead provided me with some great stories about Fox during their days with the New York Giants.

And Sam Mills has been a treasure to the Panthers since the day he arrived in Charlotte, both as a player and a coach. I have enjoyed interviewing him countless times over the years and greatly appreciate him making time for me between rounds of chemotherapy this off season.

I would be remiss not to offer thanks to Charlie Dayton, who is the Panthers' excellent media relations director and also boasts a killer forehand. He and his fine staff—Bruce Speight, Ted Crews, Deedee Thomason and Susan Ricker—have helped me for years.

And, of course, thanks to Panthers team owner Jerry Richardson. If he hadn't dreamed big from the beginning, the Carolina Panthers would have never existed.

Many thanks to my colleagues at *The Charlotte Observer*, where I have worked as a sports reporter and columnist since 1994. Mike Persinger, Gary Schwab, Frank Barrows and Jennie Buckner have been instrumental in guiding my career for 10 years and supportive of all my work. All four have taught me not only how to write a better sentence but also how to be a better person. I appreciate both lessons.

Charles Chandler is a great *Observer* reporter and was also the best man at my wedding. He and I coauthored *Year of the Cat*—a book about the 1996 Panthers team—and having such a fine experience with that book made me want to write this one.

Pat Yasinskas, Stan Olson and Paul Domeier are all gifted colleagues who know the Panthers inside and out and helped lead the coverage of the 2003 team for the newspaper. Tom Sorensen, my fellow sports columnist at the newspaper, is a superb writer who has always been extremely easy to work with and a great friend.

The sports department at my newspaper is a wonderful place to work. The sports desk and the design team has invariably treated my work with respect and patience. Harry Pickett has been a godsend to the entire sports staff from well before the time I arrived. And without Mark Hames, my laptop computer would have died many painful deaths already.

The photo desk at *The Observer* agreed to supply all the photos for this book, and for that I owe many people thanks, among them Peter Weinberger, Phil Hoffman, Patrick Schneider, Jeff Siner and David Foster III. A special thanks to Chris Record, a talented photographer who took many of the pictures for this book and also went far beyond the call sorting through old Panther photos on his own time to make sure I had everything I needed.

Thanks to my sister, Mary Lawson, and to my parents, Abby and Steve Fowler, who have always believed in me.

Thanks to my in-laws, Jim and Frances Mundy, whose babysitting help and unquestioned support were so key during this project.

Thanks to Susan Burdine and Jan Francis—two of the finest teachers ever.

Thanks to Erik Witten, who made sure I didn't stay inside hunched over a computer for months on end without a break, and to Basil Kane, who offered invaluable advice and friendship.

And, of course, thanks to Jim Fair, who was the best mentor a teenaged sportswriter just starting out in the business in my hometown of Spartanburg, South Carolina, could have ever had.

Introduction

Iremember the exact moment that I knew the Carolina Panthers were ripe for a book. It was a dreamlike moment, vivid and strange—a few seconds after a Panthers playoff game entered its *sixth* quarter.

I was in St. Louis for the Carolina/St. Louis divisional playoff game on January 10, 2004. The game was tied at 23-all. I had covered more than 100 Panther games in my sportswriting career for *The Charlotte Observer*, following every move the team made since its very first game in 1995.

Already, no matter how this one turned out, I knew it was the most extraordinary Panthers game ever played.

The crowd in St. Louis was louder than one at a Bruce Springsteen concert. Despite their screamed wishes, the underdog Panthers had surged ahead, 23-12, only to see the Rams storm back with 11 straight points in the fourth quarter. Both teams had seemingly moved into position to win the game in the first overtime, only to miss field goals.

With the game still tied, the Panthers faced third and 14 from their own 31 as the second overtime began and Carolina's destiny peeked around the corner.

In the past 17 years, no NFL game had gone on as long as this one. This was the 15th round of a heavyweight fight, and the Panthers were on the ropes. They were literally wearing down. Quarterback Jake Delhomme had gotten sacked on three of the past five pass plays. Linebacker Dan Morgan's body was throbbing with cramps on the sideline.

The St. Louis home crowd was hoarse but catching a second wind. It appeared that the Rams were about to get the ball back after a Panthers punt.

The Panthers called a play named "X Clown," in which wide receiver Steve Smith pretends to run toward the sideline and then tries to split the safeties by cutting inside. Smith had messed the play up at least 10 times during practice that week.

But this time, he ran it perfectly.

The offensive line gave Delhomme time to throw. Smith faked out St. Louis safety Jason Sehorn so badly that Sehorn never touched Smith on the play.

Delhomme fired the most famous pass of his life. Smith grabbed it at the 50.

"I braced myself for the big hit, but it never came," Smith said. "And when I took off, I knew I was gone."

Smith ran into the end zone, both arms outstretched, looking straight up at the domed ceiling.

Smith's famous pose, he would say later in an interview for this book, wasn't all about self-glorification.

"When I did that," Smith said, "it was to say, 'Wow! Look at us!' Not look at me—look at us. What do you think about us now?"

The stadium went stone silent—except for a small band of Panther players who mobbed Smith and a few hundred Carolina fans exulting in one end zone.

It was at that moment I thought to myself: This is amazing. It has to be time for a Panthers book.

You're holding in your hands what resulted. *Tales from the Carolina Panthers Sideline* chronicles the memorable characters and the behind-the-scenes stories of the 2003 Panthers team, which eventually won the NFC title and sped to the Super Bowl before losing a thriller to New England.

Whether you like to read in small sips or big gulps, you should be set. Each of the 14 chapters in this book is divided into numerous smaller stories ranging in length from 50-500 words. Each story has its own subheading to make it easy to identify the beginning and end of the tale.

So if you're the sort of person who likes to use the "random" button on your CD player, just pick up this book and haphazardly thumb through it. You're going to find a good story anywhere, even if you only have two minutes to spare.

If you prefer a more linear approach, just start at the beginning and keep going. I promise not to lose you along the way.

Chapters 1-9 detail the enchanted season of 2003, when Carolina picked up the nickname "The Cardiac Cats" because of the Panthers' knack for winning in the final minute.

If you're a fan of Jake Delhomme or Steve Smith or John Fox, you're in luck. You will find a separate chapter on each of those men here, full of things you never knew about them.

Delhomme, Smith and Coach Fox all granted exclusive interviews to me for this book. Those chapters are largely based on those interviews—although their friends and teammates have a lot to say about them too, and those stories are also included.

But this book isn't just the story of the Panthers' 2003 season.

You will also find tales of the most entertaining moments of the Panthers' first eight seasons in Chapters 10-12. And the 14th and final chapter, called "Weird Stuff," is one of my favorites. It contains stories about extreme Panther fans, about the crab claw that once gave Jordan Gross an accidental tongue piercing at dinner and about many other things that were too offbeat to make their way into one of the other chapters.

Many of those pre-2003 Panther seasons can be summed up by one of the all-time best Panther quotes. It was uttered by distraught head coach George Seifert, shortly after Carolina had managed to blow a 24-6 lead against Buffalo and lose, 25-24, in 2001.

"The problem here is that we haven't solved the problem," Seifert said. "And it's been an ongoing problem."

Exactly.

But even the Panthers' problems produced fine (and sometimes painful) storytelling moments. And there were two sensational years among those first eight seasons that absolutely deserved and received their own chapter. The 1995 squad, Carolina's first ever team, is explored in Chapter 10. The 1996 team, which went 13-5 and advanced all the way to the NFC Championship game, is documented in Chapter 11.

That 1996 Carolina team holds a special place in many Panther fans' hearts. I remember it fondly as well. That team's success led to my first book, co-written with my *Charlotte Observer* colleague Charles Chandler and called *Year of the Cat.*

I have long joked with people since that I could have written many Panther sequels since then, all of them entitled *Year of the Dog.* But finally, the 2003 Panthers team emerged and ensured Carolina would be taken seriously again.

I also owe a special debt to Sam Mills.

From the moment Mills joined the Panthers in 1995, taking a chance on a team that had never played a game, the linebacker added a dose of class to the Panthers. There was no more fitting choice than Mills as the first player to be honored with a statue outside the team's stadium and membership in the Panthers Hall of Honor.

Mills was a joy to write about and to interview as a player—self-deprecating, insightful and a man who played like he was grateful for every Sunday God gave him. I have long considered him a friend.

Like so many fans in the Carolinas and men in the NFL, I grieved when the Panthers announced in August 2003 that Mills had colon cancer. At that time, Mills would later reveal in an interview for this book, that doctors were privately bracing Mills for the possibility that he would die before New Year's Day 2004.

But Mills fought his way into 2004, still holding onto his job as the Panthers' linebackers coach and making it to the Super Bowl for the first time ever.

Mills was kind enough to spend a few hours with me in March 2004, describing his battle against cancer and his notable playing career. That interview forms the foundation of Chapter 13: "Forever Sam Mills."

Lastly, and most importantly, I want to thank Panthers fans for caring enough to read about this team so religiously for the past decade. Without you I wouldn't have my regular job as a sports columnist for *The Charlotte Observer*, and this book would never exist.

I hope you enjoy the stories told here. Thanks for reading.

Chapter 1

The Delhomme Factor

The Carolina Panthers have had seven starting quarterbacks in their brief history. But Jake Delhomme is absolutely unique.

He's not the most accurate—that was Steve Beuerlein. He's not the one who was a No. 1 draft choice—that was Kerry Collins. He's not the one with the strongest arm—that is Chris Weinke.

Delhomme, however, is easily the coolest quarterback under pressure the Panthers have ever employed.

"The bigger the game, the bigger he gets," Panthers coach John Fox often says of Delhomme.

Delhomme also boasts one of the most colorful backgrounds a Panther has ever had. He's a Cajun hailing from Breaux Bridge, Louisiana, the self-proclaimed "Crawfish Capital of the World."

And, most importantly, Delhomme is the only one who ever quarterbacked the Panthers to a Super Bowl.

Starting with the second half of the 2003 season, Delhomme morphed into a creator in the Panthers offense rather than a caretaker. His fourth-quarter, game-winning drives

*After the playoff win against Dallas in January 2004, a jubilant Jake Delhomme circled the stadium with his teammates, slapping hands with fans. At some point, a fan put a strand of Mardi Gras beads around Delhomme's neck. "I don't even know who it was who gave me the beads, but I liked them," Delhomme said. (Photo by Patrick Schneider/*The Charlotte Observer*)*

became the stuff of legend in a single season. As the Panthers' coaches grew to trust their mop-topped quarterback more, they opened up the offense and allowed Delhomme to win or lose games for them at the end.

Time after time, he won.

Even the Super Bowl loss can hardly be blamed on Delhomme, who surely would have been the Super Bowl MVP had Carolina won. He threw for 211 yards in the fourth quarter alone, including an 85-yard touchdown pass to Muhsin Muhammad that was the longest play from scrimmage in Super Bowl history. On each of Carolina's final three offensive drives, Delhomme led the team to a touchdown.

I spent many hours with Delhomme during the season and also made a trip to Breaux Bridge and Lafayette, Louisiana, to better understand his roots. What I've found out is Delhomme is a person whom Panther fans would like just as much if he were their next-door neighbor. He's that nice of a guy, genuinely unaffected by success—and you would understand why if you met his parents and his family.

After not landing an NFL starting job until age 28, Delhomme also has emerged as an NFL star. No. 17 will be leading Carolina's fourth-quarter drives down the field for years to come because he signed a five-year, $38 million contract extension in June 2004. And Panthers fans will always remember 2003, the season that started it all for Delhomme.

Ice, Ice Baby

For his 2003 Christmas party for the Carolina offense, Panthers center Jeff Mitchell was trying to figure out something unique to do.

"Kevin Donnalley told me we had to have karaoke," Mitchell said. "And I was like, 'You're either crazy or on crack, Kevin. We're not having any karaoke.'"

Donnalley persisted, though, and Mitchell eventually came around. Mitchell hired a deejay who specialized in karaoke to come to his house.

And who was the eventual star of the Panthers' karaoke show?

Jake Delhomme.

"Not only does Jake know know every single word of "Ice, Ice Baby" by Vanilla Ice, but he also knew every dance step," Mitchell said. "It was amazing. And somewhat scary."

Donnalley filmed Delhomme's performance with the video camera he carried around for most of the 2003 season, making sure the moment was saved for posterity.

While most of the reviews of Delhomme's performance were good, wide receiver Steve Smith also saw it and offered a differing opinion.

"Remember the Asian guy on *American Idol* who was so terrible that they kept playing the clip over and over?" Smith said. "That was Jake."

The Jacksonville Splash

Long before "Ice, Ice Baby," the Panthers and their fans learned how cool Delhomme really was.

Delhomme's first moment of fame as a Panther came in his very first game on September 7, 2003. Without his performance against Jacksonville in the season opener, his entire career at Carolina would have turned out differently.

After Carolina fell behind 14-0 in the first half with 2002 starting quarterback Rodney Peete at the helm, the Panthers were actually booed off the field. At home! In the first game of the season!

Coach John Fox, making quite possibly the most important decision of the season, thought he had to do something different. He told offensive coordinator Dan Henning to tell

Delhomme to get ready. Henning relayed the news to Delhomme right in front of the quarterback's locker. Henning simply pointed at Delhomme and said, "You're in."

Delhomme, uncharacteristically, didn't say anything. He just started stretching.

By the time Delhomme actually entered the game in the third quarter, Jacksonville had added another field goal and it was 17-0.

Delhomme sprinted full speed into the huddle and started pounding helmets, cursing exuberantly and claiming to the other 10 players encircling him that the Panthers could still win.

Said Panthers tight end Kris Mangum of that moment: "I'll never forget it. Jake comes in, starts slapping people on the head, throws in some high-fives and says, 'Let's roll.' You can't coach that. There are certain quarterbacks who walk into a room and people just rally around them."

"He came into that huddle," Steve Smith said, "like it was 0-0."

Immediately, Delhomme showed his enthusiasm for the game and his penchant for sticking his tongue out like Michael Jordan in the middle of most plays. Delhomme threw three touchdown passes in that magical second half. The final one, to Ricky Proehl, came on fourth and 11 from the Jacksonville 12 with 16 seconds left in the game.

The play was called "Reno"—like the gambling town in Nevada.

After Proehl caught it on his fingertips and Carolina won, 24-23, the Panthers knew they had found a jackpot in Jake.

Why No. 17?

Jake Delhomme wore No. 12 as a backup in New Orleans and at college for the Louisiana-Lafayette Ragin' Cajuns. But when he came to the Panthers in 2003, backup Randy Fasani had that number.

Faced with a choice of a new number, Delhomme chose No. 17. It was a tribute to his daughter Lauren and to his wife. Lauren was born on December 17, 2002, after Keri Delhomme went through 17 hours of labor.

Going to Breaux Bridge

The town of Breaux Bridge, Louisiana, (pop. 7,200) left an indelible mark on Jake Delhomme. It remains his off-season sanctuary. Delhomme returns there every off season, living with his wife, Keri, and small daughter, Lauren, right next door to his parents.

"I am friends with my parents," Delhomme said. "I am happy to say that I get along great with them. They are a couple of my best friends."

Jake's house used to belong to his grandfather and is very modest—it looks more like the house of a special teams player than an NFL quarterback.

Breaux Bridge, which is 127 miles west of New Orleans, is deeply immersed in its Cajun heritage. The street signs downtown are posted in both French and English. Delhomme's second cousin, Jack Dale Delhomme, is the mayor—and such a popular one that he ran unopposed in his most recent election.

"Now our French culture is celebrated," Jack Dale Delhomme said. "But when I was little and going to school at the time Jake's father was here, I remember getting punished for speaking French in the public schools."

Breaux Bridge is also the home to Houston Texans running back Domanick Davis and former Miss USA Ali Landry, who rose to prominence after her title in advertisements for Doritos.

In the Delhommes' backyard, there's a rope that once held a tire that Jake Delhomme threw footballs through. His father, Jerry, hung it there when Jake was in the fourth grade.

When I visited the Delhommes, I was struck by how committed to family they all are and how absolutely normal they all seem. One thing Jerry Delhomme always taught his boys is that you can't change what is already done—a tenet that coach John Fox also preaches.

Said Jerry Delhomme: "When something happens, it's in the past. Jake's good at understanding that. You take something from it, you get better and then you flush it."

Jake's Older Brother

The first really good athlete in the family was Jake's older brother, Jeff. Jeff was a full-scholarship wide receiver at McNeese State. Jeff was fast enough—he once ran a 4.37 in the 40-yard dash—to garner some NFL interest before he blew out his knee. Five years older and a dead ringer for Jake, Jeff lives a half-mile down the road from his parents in Breaux Bridge. He and his wife have three kids.

Jake and Jeff still throw to each other in the backyard in the off season, allowing Jake to keep his arm in shape. "He doesn't make me run around," Jeff said. "I stay still in one spot, and he scrambles around and fires it to me."

Jeff is a painting contractor and heavily involved in his children's upbringing, and he remains a tough guy.

Jake warned all his family he wanted them nowhere near Philadelphia for the NFC Championship game—he had heard too many stories about how rough the Eagles fans are.

Jeff went anyway with a friend.

"It was something else," he said.

Jeff didn't get into a fight. But among the things he saw was one beefy relative of a Panther swimming into a pile of Eagles fans who had been tormenting the Panthers' fans and knocking the Eagles' supporters around, one by one, until they quit messing with him and anyone else nearby wearing black and blue.

A Student of Horses

A little farther back at the Delhomme compound in Breaux Bridge is the barn where Jake, Jeff and father Jerry run a small stable and train thoroughbreds together. It is not a high-dollar operation. The Delhommes prefer to buy horses for $7,500 or so in the smaller "claiming" races at the nearby Louisiana tracks and then see if they can improve the horse's performance.

Jake loves the horses. During football season, he keeps up with all of the Delhomme horses via a website called "Equibase.com."

"I don't really like to hunt and fish, and I don't really like to play golf," Jake says. "I like the horses."

Says Jake's father, Jerry: "You know Jake. He's very impatient sometimes. He'll call up the workout times on one of the horses and he'll get mad. Then he calls me up and screams, 'Get rid of that son of a gun!' I say, 'But Jake, c'mon. You want to win the Kentucky Derby the very first time out?'

"I don't want to hear it!" Jake says. "Get rid of him!"

The elder Delhomme usually is able to calm his son down, but it takes a few minutes.

"He's always had passion," Jerry Delhomme says.

Seabiscuit

Because of Jake Delhomme's love of horses and his underdog status, a number of people have compared him to the horse Seabiscuit. Delhomme loved the movie. On the Panthers' charter plane to the Super Bowl, when the movie was announced as *Seabiscuit*, Delhomme leaped over tight end Kris Mangum to get to the headphones first.

Delhomme said he does see some similarities in the stories, although he doesn't think he's won enough yet to inspire a movie.

"Sometimes, if you're not the tallest guy or don't have the strongest arm, you get pushed off to the side," Delhomme said. "But sometimes, the underdog wins. Sometimes, the underdog has the biggest heart out there."

High School Days

Jake went to Teurlings Catholic High School in nearby Lafayette, Louisiana. He won the starting quarterback job there as a freshman, played on a couple of bad teams and willed the team to victory a number of times. His favorite coach from that time still works at the school—Sonny Charpentier, who coached Delhomme in both football and basketball.

"Jake could dunk," Charpentier said. "People say he's not a great athlete.... I've been in coaching 24 years. Jake's a very good athlete but not the best one I've ever coached. But he's the most competitive player I've ever had."

Charpentier said Delhomme has never been very good at losing.

"He doesn't play golf because it's a humbling game," Charpentier laughed, "and Jake can't stand being humbled."

Said Mayor Delhomme of Jake: "That son of a gun—he'll blow up on you now and he blew up on people then."

Delhomme, whose 1993 high school graduating class numbered only 44 (including Jake and his future wife, Keri), played both ways for Teurlings. He actually made All-State as a senior as a defensive back but not as a quarterback, because a future LSU player named Josh Booty got most of the headlines.

In one game Charpentier remembers well, Delhomme threw for more than 400 yards, grabbed two interceptions, kicked a field goal and then blocked the other team's possible game-winning field goal in the final seconds.

When Delhomme was a 165-pound senior, he helped his squad get to the state semifinals before Teurlings lost.

That loss still haunts Delhomme. Immediately after the Super Bowl, he said the only loss he could compare the Super Bowl to was the one he suffered in the state semifinals as a high school senior.

"A win would have sent us to the Superdome for the finals," Delhomme says now, "and that's what every high school football player in Louisiana dreams of. I know it wasn't as big as losing the Super Bowl. No way. But that was the first thing that popped into my mind after the Super Bowl loss. I started there for four years in high school and played with four or five guys I was really close to all that time. It really hurt."

Backing Up Warner

Jake Delhomme says his lowest moment in football wasn't when he went undrafted in 1997. It wasn't when the New Orleans Saints fired him on three separate occasions.

It was when he had to sit on the bench in Amsterdam.

In 1998, Delhomme went to NFL Europe, hoping to improve his stock. But he couldn't even start—Amsterdam stuck this guy named Kurt Warner in front of him.

"I said to myself, 'C'mon, man. Let's be real. If you can't start here, how are you ever going to start in the NFL?'" Delhomme recounted once.

Of course, Warner ended up being a two-time NFL MVP.

Warner and Delhomme remain close and are represented by the same agency. But it was ironic during the Panthers' 2003 playoff run that Delhomme started for Carolina during the Panthers' upset win in St. Louis, while Warner sat on the bench and watched first-stringer Marc Bulger play for the Rams.

"We Want Jake!"

If New Orleans Saints head coach Jim Haslett had made a different decision on December 29, 2002, Jake Delhomme might never have become a Panther.

As usual, Delhomme had watched that entire season from the Saints bench as quarterback Aaron Brooks played his consistently inconsistent style. The Saints needed to win their final game that season to make the playoffs. Carolina, at 6-9, was going nowhere.

But neither were Brooks and the New Orleans offense, stifled time and again by the Panthers defense (which would finish that 2002 season ranked No. 2 in the NFL).

The chant started coming out of the Superdome stands in the second half, louder and louder as the game went on: "We want Jake! We want Jake!"

Panthers coach John Fox heard it. Delhomme heard it. Everybody heard it.

But Haslett ignored it.

If Delhomme had been inserted and had won that game for New Orleans, who knows what would have happened? Perhaps the Saints would have had a 2002 postseason run to rival Carolina's in 2003 and Delhomme would have become the new starter for New Orleans.

Instead, Brooks stayed in.

Carolina won the game, 10-6.

New Orleans didn't make the playoffs.

And Delhomme became a Panther.

The (Temporarily) Quiet Man

Jake Delhomme is a passionate player whom teammates occasionally liken to Bobby Boucher—the fictional Cajun portrayed by Adam Sandler in the 1998 movie *The Waterboy.*

*This Delhomme celebration came not after a touchdown pass, but after a Stephen Davis TD run against New Orleans in October 2003. Said offensive guard Kevin Donnalley: "Jake seems to be just fiery and passionate and doesn't care how it gets done. He just wants to get it done." (Photo by Patrick Schneider/*The Charlotte Observer*)*

Delhomme doesn't particularly like the analogy, in part because the movie often makes fun of Cajuns, and Sandler's character speaks almost unintelligibly. Delhomme will occasionally play a game with himself and try to conduct an entire interview without gesturing with his hands—wide receiver Ricky Proehl once teased him and said he couldn't do it.

But no one really knew much about Delhomme's screaming passion for the game during Training Camp 2003, his first with Carolina.

First of all, he often looked terrible. It's hard to celebrate when you're throwing interceptions. And of all the quarterbacks in camp, Delhomme looked the worst early on. Everyone else had experience in Dan Henning's offense. Delhomme didn't.

I talked to Delhomme right in the middle of his 800-mile drive from Louisiana to Charlotte in the summer of 2003 and asked him what he thought his chances to start were. His reply was careful.

"I would think I can," Delhomme said. "I'd love to be the starter on opening day. But I don't know if that's going to happen or not—if I'm going to have enough time. If Rodney Peete turns out to be the guy, he deserves it."

When Delhomme got to camp, he understood that most of his teammates assumed that Peete (the starter in 2002 for the Panthers' 7-9 team) would win the job again.

"I don't think my teammates believed in me at all back then," Delhomme said. "And you know what? They shouldn't have. I had never done anything for anybody, basically. So I worked hard, was very quiet, tried to be a nice guy and tried real hard not to get in the way."

No More (Re)Peetes

Jake Delhomme's ascension to stardom in the Jacksonville game basically wrested the controls away from Rodney Peete for the rest of the season. Peete, a 15-year veteran, had had a respectable year in 2002. But he gracefully assumed the role of backup, even letting Delhomme's family use the Peete luxury suite occasionally for Carolina home games.

"It would be easy to be that guy who's angry and disruptive, but I'm too old for that," Peete said.

Delhomme admired Peete both for his knowledge of the game and his knowledge of America's celebrities. Thanks in large part to his wife, TV actress Holly Robinson Peete (who had large roles in *21 Jump Street* and *Hangin' With Mr. Cooper*), Rodney has become cordial with many famous people.

For instance, the Peetes' wedding was officiated by Rev. Jesse Jackson.

"There is not a person that Rodney Peete doesn't know," Delhomme said. "It's kind of funny. I mean any big name, they see Rodney and they come and give him a hug. He's Mr. Hollywood."

Another example? The night before Peete's first game as a Panther in 2002, Peete picked up his phone and heard the voice of an old friend wishing him good luck.

The friend: Bill Clinton.

Peete's second cousin is golfer Calvin Peete. His father, Willie Peete, is a retired NFL running backs coach. His father-in-law, Matthew Robinson, was the original "Gordon" on *Sesame Street* and later became one of the principal writers for *The Cosby Show*.

How Do You Say That, Anyway?

Delhomme's last name is of French heritage, as most of the last names in Cajun country are. Loosely translated, it means "The Man"—a fitting surname for a quarterback.

But how to pronounce it? Broadcasters had all sorts of trouble early in the 2003 season. "I've been called just about everything," Delhomme said.

For the record, as any Panther fan knows, you say it "duh-LOME."

A Close Relationship

Carolina center Jeff Mitchell is one of the Panthers' funniest players. With Jake Delhomme's hands on Mitchell's rear end before every play, Mitchell has also had more contact with Delhomme than most of the Panthers ever will.

When asked how he would characterize his relationship with Delhomme, Mitchell joked: "It is definitely intimate."

Keeping the Linemen Happy

One of Delhomme's best attributes is his ability to get along with his offensive linemen, who control so much of what goes on during every offensive possession.

Said Jordan Gross, who started as a rookie at right tackle all season in 2003: "When we are doing well, Jake is our biggest fan. When something goes wrong, he looks to himself. He never points fingers."

Said Kevin Donnalley, who started the entire 2003 season at right guard beside Gross: "Jake is just generally a positive person. He always believes you can win it until the end. You never see defeat on his face."

Continued Donnalley: "I know early on, everyone was thinking, 'OK, this guy has won a few games for us, this is great. But sooner or later, he might come down to reality.' But it never happened. I think what made him so good for us is he'd come back to the huddle after throwing an interception or near-interception and he'd say, 'Hey fellas, I don't know what happened. That was the stupidest thing I've ever done. I suck, but I'm going to keep on fighting.' And you're like, all right!

"Or Jake would say right before we needed a game-winning drive: 'Hey, guys, I know I'm going to get time here. Look at my jersey. It's clean. I haven't been touched all day. I can do this. I'm going to make this play. We're going to win this.'

"Most quarterbacks I've played with—and I've blocked for Warren Moon and Dan Marino—aren't like that," Donnalley said. "Marino would chew you out when something went wrong, but he was always very cool and calculating. Jake seems to be just fiery and passionate and doesn't care how it gets done. He just wants to get it done."

High Praise from the Greats

Former New York Giants star quarterback Phil Simms was the lead analyst for the Panthers-Patriots Super Bowl, and he believes that Jake Delhomme and two-time Super Bowl MVP Tom Brady share many of the same qualities.

"One of Tom Brady's coaches told me that every coach on the New England staff thinks he is Brady's best friend," Simms said. "And he does that with the players, too. That is a tough quality to find in today's NFL quarterbacks. About one-third of them have no personality, and they do nothing for the team."

Continued Simms: "I don't know Jake well, but I think he's got a lot of the same qualities as Brady. A huddle is like a restaurant, really. You've got to work the room. You want the guys to perform for you? Work the room, baby."

Former Miami Dolphins quarterback Dan Marino also is a fan of Delhomme's.

"You know what I love about him?" Marino asked me. "He stands in there when the game's on the line and makes throws. Even when he gets blitzed, he stands right in there."

Marino also said that Delhomme's trademark rainbow throw—the one he made so often in 2003 to Steve Smith and Muhsin Muhammad—was a good weapon that not enough quarterbacks used.

"If you've got the right receivers that you can trust," Marino said, "it's a great weapon. I used to do it myself sometimes—especially with Mark Clayton and Mark Duper."

A Special Connection

Jake Delhomme and Panthers wide receiver Steve Smith have a special bond, one that started developing in the early days of the Panthers' 2003 training camp in Spartanburg, South Carolina. Both are naturally impatient. Smith will break a route off if he thinks something isn't working, and Delhomme likes to get the ball out quickly. They found their natural styles suited each other.

By late in the season, after Smith had hauled in the 69-yard touchdown pass from Delhomme at St. Louis to win that double-overtime playoff game, the two had suddenly become famous.

I was on Tony Kornheiser's old ESPN radio show just before the Panthers played Philadelphia in the NFC Championship game. While predicting a Panthers win—Kornheiser disagreed with me, incidentally—I mentioned Delhomme and Smith.

Kornheiser then said something fairly remarkable.

"I'm totally serious about this," Kornheiser said. "For the last few weeks, those two have been playing like Montana and Rice."

Delhomme has only known Smith since Smith has matured a bit. Delhomme wasn't on the team when Smith committed the awful offense of hitting his own teammate, Anthony Bright, in a team meeting. That probably helps.

"He is a good person," Delhomme said of Smith. "There has been so much made of him being a ticking time bomb, but he's not. Not at all."

*Undrafted out of college, Delhomme only had two starts in six NFL seasons before joining the Panthers at age 28. "Sometimes, if you're not the tallest guy or don't have the strongest arm, you get pushed off to the side," Delhomme said. "But sometimes, the underdog wins. Sometimes, the underdog has the biggest heart out there." Delhomme is shown here in action against Jacksonville in the 2003 season opener, when he entered the game with Carolina trailing, 17-0, and led the Panthers to a 24-23 win. (Photo by Patrick Schneider/*The Charlotte Observer*)*

In early 2004, I called Delhomme in Louisiana and asked him what he thought of Smith signing a new long-term contract with Carolina that should keep the two together for years.

"I told my wife when I heard about it," Delhomme said, "that I'm going to sleep really well tonight."

Chapter 2

Birth of the Cardiac Cats

The Carolina Panthers arrived in Spartanburg in the summer of 2003 without really knowing what sort of team they would be. History said it wouldn't be very good—the Panthers boasted only one winning season in their eight-year history.

But there was some optimism. After suffering through a nasty eight-game losing streak in 2002, Carolina had rebounded to win four of its final five games.

This was a team so far under the national radar in the summer of 2003 that they wouldn't play a single game on *Monday Night Football*—as usual. Their only game in prime time would be against Atlanta in December, and that was only because Michael Vick played for the other team.

Carolina, in other words, was about as ignored a team as you could be in the NFL.

All that would change, however, for the team that would eventually become known as the "Cardiac Cats."

Here are some of the most memorable tales from both the 2003 training camp and Carolina's first five games of that season, when the Panthers started 5-0 and quickly showed the NFL that ignoring them would be perilous.

The Rap-Off

For every NFL team, training camp is something of a return to a high school. For the most part, no wives, girlfriends or children are around. The locker-room humor is adolescent. The players' lives are as uncluttered as they will be all year. Only football matters.

It is no different for the Carolina Panthers, who have trained since their inception in Spartanburg, South Carolina, the hometown of team owner Jerry Richardson.

Spartanburg is a sleepy town compared to Charlotte. I know this well, since I grew up there myself. This is exactly the way the Panthers like it. They don't want their players getting into trouble in training camp. And while that hasn't always worked—quarterback Kerry Collins was a notable exception back in his wilder days—it usually does.

The Panthers find various ways to amuse themselves between coach John Fox's notoriously fierce two-a-day practices. Among them are "rap-offs," which are conducted in the locker room.

In a rap-off, an instrumental rap beat is played on somebody's CD player. Then two players face off, one at a time, doing freelance lyrics designed to insult the other player.

One of the rap-off champions in the summer of 2003 was Terrance Simmons. Simmons was never much of a player for the Panthers, getting in only two games during his brief career. He had great size at 6-8, 328 pounds, but the team never could figure out whether he should play on offense or defense.

But Simmons could rap—"This dude rapped all the time," remembered Mike Rucker—and he would accept a challenge from anyone.

One day defensive tackle Brentson Buckner, who loved to watch the rap-offs but never participated, decided to challenge Simmons. At that point, Simmons had recently been switched back to the offensive line.

Remembered Buckner: "The way those things work, you want the crowd to go crazy at the very end. You save your best lines for last so he won't really have a chance. Now Terrance was a nice guy, but it was hard to understand sometimes what he was saying. And of course he never could really find a position. So my last two lines were: 'What you saying doesn't make no sense. If you was any good on this team they would have kept you on defense.'"

The other players yowled, and Buckner was rap king for the day.

Don't Slam the...

Buckner was also one of the team's occasional pranksters in Spartanburg. The players stay in dorm-style rooms on the Wofford College campus, and the atmosphere is collegial.

"Toward the end of camp, a lot of guys don't even lock their doors," Buckner said. "The team is always doing bed checks, and it's just easier for them to check on you that way without you having to ever wake up. So me and Deon Grant used to go around when some of the other guys went to sleep early. All you needed on one of those doors was to slam it from about seven inches out and it would make an incredible noise— it felt like it would bust your eardrums. It would not only scare the people in the room, it would scare people down the hall. One night, we got [tight end] Jermaine Wiggins good. We ran off and I think he stayed in there all night, afraid that somebody was going to get him."

A Sudden Respect

The first thing many players noticed in the summer of 2003 was that Carolina's offense looked a lot better. In 2002, the Panthers' defense had gotten all the publicity—it ranked second in the NFL, while the Panthers' offense was a woeful 31st.

"We were an also-ran in 2002," said Kevin Donnalley, who started for the Panthers at offensive guard from 2001 through 2003. "Our own defense made fun of us behind our backs. In 2002, there was trash-talking, fights—just some general punking of the offense during camp. But early in the 2003 camp you knew it was going to be different. There were hardly any fights. There was much more respect. With Stephen Davis and Jake Delhomme and Jordan Gross and the other additions, the defense could tell we were going to be better."

Said Brentson Buckner, who admitted to being part of the "punking" of the offense in 2002: "That's totally accurate. In 2002, it was so easy for us. We're all competitive, and in training camp, the only people you can compete against is your own team. So in 2002, we would be like, 'We don't want them to get a yard today.' And they wouldn't get a yard. Or Jack Del Rio [the defensive coordinator in 2002] would tell us we need five turnovers today, and we'd go get six or seven.

"But then," Buckner continued, "they went out and got Stephen Davis. And it was like the offensive line said, 'Hey, we've got a proven guy who's going to be behind us. No. 48 is going to make us look good.' And it got a lot harder. On some days in training camp, they just destroyed us."

Grossly Exaggerated

One of Stephen Davis's key blockers throughout the entire 2003 season was rookie right tackle Jordan Gross, and the acquisition of Gross is a story in itself.

For that pickup, the Carolina Panthers owe the Minnesota Vikings a favor. The Panthers may have never gotten Gross—a starter from day one during his time with Carolina—if not for a Vikings mistake.

Picking No. 9 that day in April 2003, Carolina coveted Gross. Minnesota had the No. 7 overall choice. The Vikings were trying to trade down with Baltimore (choosing No. 10).

But Minnesota didn't turn in its trade card in the 15-minute time allotment. Quickly, Jacksonville (originally choosing eighth, but now with an opportunity to be No. 7) grabbed Marshall quarterback Byron Leftwich. Then Carolina speedily turned in its own draft card to grab Gross at No. 8—the player Jacksonville likely would have selected had the Jaguars not already gotten Leftwich.

A sheepish Minnesota wound up picking No. 9. Gross—who allowed no sacks as a Utah senior and had 129 knockdown blocks—became a Panther.

The Hardest Days

The Panthers' most difficult days of the 2003 season came before a real game was ever played.

Standout linebacker Mark Fields played in Carolina's first exhibition game, against Washington. He jammed his thumb and had to get it worked on a little by doctors.

"He's getting his thumb drained," coach John Fox said at the time. "It's not a major injury."

But Fields's thumb wouldn't heal, and this was rare. He was graced with a great body, one durable enough that he had missed only six games total in an eight-year NFL career.

So Fields checked into a hospital and got some tests done.

It turned out he had Hodgkin's disease.

His linebackers coach, Sam Mills, called Fields at the hospital to check on his star player's injured thumb.

"Coach, you won't believe what they laid on me today," Fields said softly. "They said I have cancer."

"Cancer?!" Mills said. He was speechless.

"At that time, I didn't know hardly anything about cancer," Mills would say months later in an interview for this book. "I didn't really know what to say. Kinda ironic, isn't it?"

Fields's cancer would force him to miss the entire 2003 season.

Fields immediately pledged to eventually continue his career. The Panthers, meanwhile, pledged to pay his full salary.

"I Feel Good!"

One of my favorite Fields stories came in 2002, when he was arguably the Panthers' most valuable player. Fields had missed a game—the only one he would miss that season—with a groin injury. Reporters asked him if he'd play the next week and how he was feeling.

Fields lifted a finger to his lips in a "Shhh" sign, then led reporters to a James Brown doll in his locker. Then he pressed a button on the doll, and suddenly James Brown's voice screeched: "I Feeeeel Gooood!!!"

A lot of people thought of that doll when Fields was originally diagnosed, hoping that he'd be able to play the same trick again once he returned to the playing field in 2004.

The Worst Press Release Ever

Only two weeks after Mark Fields was diagnosed with cancer, the Panthers handed out a press release on August 29, 2003, just before an exhibition game with Pittsburgh.

It was only 25 words long, and read like this: "Carolina Panthers linebacker coach Sam Mills has been diagnosed with cancer of the small intestine. At this time, Sam's treatment and work schedule are undetermined."

Mills's work schedule for that night was already determined, though—by Mills.

Showing the determination that had always marked his NFL career, Mills worked the game that night with the other defensive coaches from the press box. He had his doctor drive him straight to the stadium from the hospital. Mills ended up working the entire season, despite the fact that he underwent three full days of chemotherapy every two weeks. (Chapter 13 of this book is devoted entirely to Mills—the player, the coach and the cancer patient).

The players already knew about Mills's cancer that August evening, and they were devastated. Coach John Fox had told them about both Fields and Mills in separate team meetings, two weeks apart.

"We learned about Mark in training camp," Kevin Donnalley said. "Coach Fox made the announcement and talked to the team. He said right away it was very, very serious, but that it was one of the most treatable forms of cancer. That kind of prepared us for the Sam Mills announcement two weeks later. Because it wasn't the same demeanor. Without a word, I think everybody knew, 'Hey, Sam is a whole lot more serious. We really need to circle the wagons now.'"

Proehl's Project

With the diagnoses of Sam Mills and Mark Fields fresh on the minds of the Panthers, no one knew how they would play in their first game of the 2003 season.

Thanks to a big assist from new Panther Ricky Proehl, they won it, 24-23, against Jacksonville.

*The game-winning touchdown in Carolina's first game of 2003 came on a play called "Reno." The Panthers had the play more than 100 times in practice over the summer, and the ball hadn't gone to Proehl once. (Photo by Jeff Siner/*The Charlotte Observer*)*

It had taken Ricky Proehl years to get inside the Panthers' stadium in one way.

In another, though, he had been there forever.

Proehl, the veteran wide receiver, was a charter permanent-seat license holder for the first season in what was then known as Ericsson Stadium. That was in 1996.

He never got to use his own tickets, because he was always busy Sunday playing somewhere else. But he figured that at some point, once he retired, he would enjoy making the 90-minute drive from Greensboro to Charlotte for the games.

While Proehl is originally from New Jersey, he went to Wake Forest and met his wife there. The family has since settled near where Proehl went to college.

Proehl finally made it to the stadium—as a player—in 2003. The Panthers signed him to be their slot receiver, and on his first real game ever as part of the home team he made that signing look very good.

Proehl made the winning touchdown catch against Jacksonville in the 2003 season opener, finger-tipping a fourth-down, 12-yard touchdown pass from Jake Delhomme with 16 seconds left that began the Panthers' Super Bowl season and also jump-started the Delhomme legend. It was also the 50th touchdown catch of Proehl's career, counting the playoffs.

What most people don't realize about that play is that the Panthers had run it more than 100 times during the 2003 training camp and the ball hadn't gone to Proehl once.

But this time Delhomme looked for Muhsin Muhammad, didn't like what he saw, glanced at Steve Smith cutting over the middle and quickly scanned the field again.

Proehl had gone in motion to the left, frozen a linebacker with one cut and then faked out a cornerback with another. He leaped for Delhomme's pass, caught it and then took the ball to his PSL seats in the stands. Proehl found his eight-year-old son, Austin, handed him the ball and said, "This one is for you."

Out of the Stands

Jake Delhomme's enthusiasm in that first game caught some of the players off guard. Delhomme really hadn't played much with the first team in the preseason, so his helmet-bashing and constant Cajun chatter surprised many in the huddle.

Said center Jeff Mitchell: "I often compare him to somebody they just pulled out of the stands to play. It is like he is surprised and happy just to be out there. It is like the first time every time. That's the sense I get from him."

Although listed six foot two and 215 pounds, Delhomme looks both skinnier and younger in person.

"It's like he's a Little League kid out there," Mitchell laughed. "I mean, look at him. He's about 150 pounds and you'd swear he's about 12 years old. He's got those big ears and when he bounces into the huddle it's like, 'Ba-doing, ba-doing—what's up, guys!'"

When Davis Almost Quit

Stephen Davis, one of the Panthers' glistening stars of 2003, grew up in the housing projects of Spartanburg, South Carolina. The Davis place was only about 10 minutes from the training-camp fields at Wofford College where he eventually practiced during the summer with the Panthers.

But Davis very nearly never made that jump. When he was 16 years old, his mother developed breast cancer and he thought about quitting football.

Davis's mother, whose given name is really and truly Queen Elizabeth Davis, raised five children on her own. Davis was the youngest. When his mother got sick, he was confused and scared.

"I was the youngest child, and nobody was there to take care of her," Davis said. "I wanted to stay home and take care of her, but she wouldn't let me do it. Basically she said, 'No, I'm not going to let you quit. Don't you ever quit something that you've started.' That always stuck in my mind."

Queenie Davis survived her bout with breast cancer and got to see her son play a number of games in the 2003 season, including the Super Bowl.

The Blocked Extra Point

After the last-second win against Jacksonville in the season opener, Carolina was 1-0. But the Panthers were major underdogs in their next game, on September 14, 2003, against defending Super Bowl champion Tampa Bay.

Brentson Buckner had caused a preseason ripple when he said Panthers defensive tackle Kris Jenkins was better than Tampa Bay's Warren Sapp. Buckner had also said that the Panthers' defensive line as a whole was better than Tampa Bay's. This all proved to be true but seemed like heresy to many at the time, since Tampa Bay had just won the Super Bowl with a smashing defensive performance.

In this game, played on a sweltering, 91-degree afternoon, both defenses played very well. Carolina led, 9-3, deep in the fourth quarter, but Tampa Bay scored on the final play of regulation to tie the game, 9-9.

All that was left was for Tampa Bay's Martin (Automatica) Gramatica to kick an extra point for the win. Gramatica was 129 for 129 in his career on extra points.

The Panthers lined up, showing the Buccaneers one type of formation. Then coach John Fox called timeout, trying to ice Gramatica and also to throw in a tactical change.

The Panthers came back out in a different formation. Jenkins broke through the line so easily that he actually blocked Gramatica's extra point with his *elbow*.

The game went into overtime—the first of five OT games Carolina would play during the 2003 season—and the Panthers would win it, 12-9.

Said Buckner: "I think that timeout and that block was a turning point in how much we believed in Coach Fox. He had always said if you play hard to the end, you never know what is going to happen. He said it again during the timeout. And once Jenks blocked that extra point, I knew we wouldn't lose. We were going to play until the next day if we had to."

Said safety Mike Minter: "You never see something like that. A blocked extra point to decide a game? C'mon."

Said offensive tackle Jordan Gross: "In my mind, that play really kind of started the season for us."

Shrugged Jenkins: "I just blocked it. It wasn't rocket science."

The Two Biggest Games

When you ask coach John Fox now, well after the 2003 season is over, what the biggest wins of that big year were, he doesn't hesitate. He doesn't talk about playoff games. He talks about Jacksonville and Tampa Bay.

"The thing that set the tone for us was our first two games," Fox said. "Had those gone differently, it would have been more difficult. In that first half against Jacksonville, we were awful. To reach down and turn that around was big. And then when we went to Tampa and I saw the mindset and determination of our bunch, I thought we had a chance. Not just to win that game, but to be special. A special team. These were the defending champs. Nobody thought we had a prayer.

"But that day, there was no fear on our sideline. And no doubt. That was special."

The Davis Difference

When Atlanta head coach Dan Reeves was asked in 2003 what the difference between a Carolina Panther team with Stephen Davis and one without him, Reeves's reply was succinct.

"About 160 yards," Reeves said.

In fact, Davis helped contribute to Reeves's demise in Atlanta. Davis gained 153 yards in Carolina's 23-3 win over

Atlanta on September 28, 2003, pushing Carolina to a 3-0
record. Reeves and Atlanta had decimated the Panthers in 2002,
winning the two games by a combined score of 71-0.

This time, behind Davis, Carolina was far better. It also
didn't help Reeves that he was missing his own star, quarterback
Michael Vick, for that first matchup.

By the end of the season, Davis was heading to the Pro
Bowl.

Reeves had been fired.

Faster Than You'd Think

Stephen Davis is known as a hammer of a back, the kind who
will pound you incessantly. But he is also surprisingly fast.
Davis doesn't much like when people say DeShaun Foster is
Carolina's "fast" back, implying Davis must be the slow one.

In fact, while in high school in South Carolina, Davis used
to regularly defeat a kid named Tim Montgomery during the
high-school track season. Davis won the state 100-meter dash
title three times, and his record of 10.4 seconds in the 100 in
1991 remained the South Carolina state mark when he joined
the Panthers. More than a decade later, if you want to make
Davis smile, just bring up that record.

Montgomery turned into the world's fastest man.
Seriously. He set the world record in the 100-meter dash at 9.78
seconds—and also has had a baby with women's sprinting star
Marion Jones.

Davis ran those fast times before he bulked up to 230
pounds, though. Now his speed certainly helps, but his yardage
comes mostly from great vision and what his teammates refer to
as the "Davis lean." Davis always runs bent forward, as if he's on
a Chicago crosswalk facing a killer wind.

*Although Stephen Davis's major strength is his power running, he could surprise you with his speed. In high school in Spartanburg, South Carolina, Davis used to regularly defeat a kid named Tim Montgomery in track meets. Montgomery would later go on to hold the world record at 100 meters. Davis is shown here against New Orleans on October 5, 2003. (Photo by Christopher A. Record/*The Charlotte Observer*)*

Joked fullback Brad Hoover of Davis: "It's not that he's the fastest guy in the world. I don't think he is. I think I could about run faster than Stephen."

"It's hard to get a good lick on him because of that lean," Panthers defensive tackle Brentson Buckner said.

Said Jake Delhomme: "Stephen has this internal clock. He knows exactly how long he has to find a hole, when he has to hit it and how to fall forward."

Said Panthers coach John Fox about Davis in 2003: "No. 48 makes us all look smarter."

"36 Power"

Traditionally, the Panthers have had lots of trouble running out the clock. That's one reason they allowed so many comeback wins in team history—the offense rarely could cement the game.

That changed dramatically when Stephen Davis arrived. There was no better example than during Week 4 of the 2003 regular season, when Carolina was clinging to a 19-13 lead over New Orleans.

Carolina needed a first down to cinch the game and go 4-0. Offensive coordinator Dan Henning called the same play three straight times. Its name is "36 Power," and it's a simple run to Davis that featured left guard Jeno James pulling to the right to lead the charge.

Davis needed 10 yards. In three bullish cracks, he got 11.

"They knew it was coming," Kevin Donnalley said. "We blocked it up fairly well, but really Stephen just rammed it through there."

Donnalley, like the rest of the Panthers' offensive line, was at that point just coming to grips with how good Davis really was.

"I don't think we knew what we really had until the season began," Donnalley said. "Because they pampered and babied him in training camp—they do that with all the skill-position guys. They don't want to get them hurt. But then we saw how he just hammered people, and it was awesome."

Davis had also scored a touchdown earlier in the game, which he followed by doing a dance that looked like what somebody would do if he walked through a construction site.

"Just knocking the dust off," Davis grinned. "I hadn't been in the end zone in a long time."

He Hate Me

Running back/special teamer Rod Smart came up with one of pro football's most enduring nicknames—"He Hate Me"—while playing in the short-lived XFL. How did he invent it?

"I'm a genius," deadpanned Smart.

In fact, Smart would watch film occasionally, see tacklers miss him and exclaim, "He hate me! And he hate me! And he hate me!"

At Western Kentucky, where he went to college, the nickname Smart went by was "Snoop" because of his long braids.

But in the XFL, Smart had the nickname sewn on the back of his jersey, and it was about the only thing about that silly, ill-fated league that lasted. When Smart came to Carolina, the nickname followed him. Do the other players give him grief about it?

"No," Smart said. "Everyone likes me. They don't hate me."

Smart got tons of mileage from his nickname throughout the 2003 season, especially from announcers. They couldn't get enough of it.

*Rod "He Hate Me" Smart turned out to be more than just a good nickname for the Panthers. Smart returned a kickoff 100 yards for a touchdown against New Orleans and would also entertain teammates with his wild get-ups acquired from local thrift shops. (Photo by Christopher A. Record/*The Charlotte Observer*)*

When Smart returned a kickoff 100 yards for a touchdown against New Orleans on October 5, 2003, Panthers play-by-play man Bill Rosinski ended his call of the touchdown with: "He Hate Me? We love you!" ESPN liked that one so much they replayed it constantly.

The Confidence Man

Very early in the 2003 season, it was evident how confident rookie cornerback Ricky Manning would be.

Cornerbacks have to have an arrogance about them, of course. When they make a mistake, 70,000 people see it. They have to move on and forget about it.

But Manning, a third-round pick out of UCLA, didn't seem troubled about anything at the beginning of the season.

He wasn't starting but was already getting a lot of playing time as the team's third or fourth cornerback in passing situations.

In Carolina's first preseason game, against Washington, the Panthers won, 20-0. Asked how difficult it had been to play in his first NFL game, Manning proclaimed: "Actually, it wasn't that hard. It was kind of easy."

Manning didn't realize the game was difficult, in fact, until October 12, 2003, against Indianapolis. In that one, he had to guard the Colts' Marvin Harrison for much of the game. Manning did make one incredible interception in the game— picking off quarterback Peyton Manning on a flanker screen. Manning secretly enjoyed that one a lot because he and Peyton shared the same last name.

"Manning to Manning," Ricky Manning said. "I love the sound of that."

But Harrison also got the better of Manning a number of times in the game.

"The NFL just got hard," Manning said after the Panthers pulled out a 23-20 win in overtime. "Marvin Harrison is really fast."

The Two-Headed Monster

That Indianapolis game also marked the emergence of DeShaun Foster, the team's No. 2 tailback, as an able substitute for Stephen Davis when necessary.

After Davis went out with an injury, Foster gained 85 yards in 16 carries.

"We're the two-headed monster," Davis would proclaim.

That game also showed how generous Davis would be with his time for Foster. A large part of the Panthers' running success was due to the fact that Davis would teach Foster what he knew, rather than leaving him to learn on his own in hopes that Davis could hold onto all the playing time.

Some Great Ears

That win against Indianapolis was remarkable in one other aspect—the sheer noise level. In nine years of covering the Panthers, I had never heard a football stadium so loud (although the St. Louis game would surpass it in decibel level three months later). They love to play rock music over the stadium loudspeakers in Indianapolis and the crowd was shrieking all afternoon. My ears rang coming out of the stadium like I had just walked out of a Metallica concert.

Panthers safety Mike Minter's ears were good enough that day, though, that even after all the screaming he claimed that he heard one last sound after John Kasay's 47-yard field goal in overtime clinched the upset for Carolina.

"When John's kick went in," Minter said, "I could hear the shouting all the way from Charlotte."

Chapter 3

Clawing Toward the Playoffs

The Panthers' 5-0 start in 2003 wasn't an aberration. Neither was their penchant for playing extremely close games. As defensive tackle Kris Jenkins said following yet another nailbiter: "Sometimes my heart can't handle too much of the pressure."

The nickname "Cardiac Cats" was in full flower by this point. The Panthers would end up going 7-0 in the 2003 regular season in games decided by three points or less, tying the NFL record held by the 1998 Arizona Cardinals for most wins in games that close.

The final three months of the regular season weren't easy, though. The Panthers had a shot at homefield advantage in the NFC throughout the playoffs, but basically lost it with back-to-back losses against Dallas and Philadelphia in late November. Panther players vowed revenge if they saw either team again in the playoffs.

A third straight loss to Atlanta on December 7 dropped Carolina to 8-5. But the Panthers rebounded with three straight wins in the final three weeks, finishing the regular season at 11-5 and as champions of the NFC South division.

That wasn't quite good enough for a first-round bye, but it was plenty good enough for the Panthers' first playoff appearance in seven seasons. This chapter recounts some of the more striking stories from those months in late 2003 leading up to the playoffs, along with several tales about Carolina's front defensive foursome.

The Blue Submarine

One of the most important plays of the Carolina Panthers' 2003 season came October 26, 2003, in New Orleans. It was necessary in part because of the coin toss that hit somebody's foot.

The Panthers were 5-1 by this point, having gotten blown out at home by Tennessee the week before to end their five-game win streak. They were in serious danger of losing their second straight game against New Orleans—the game went into overtime tied 20-all.

That's when the Panthers' Mike Rucker and former Saint Jake Delhomme went out for the postgame coin toss. Rucker likes to call "tails" for coin tosses, because he's superstitious and says that "tails" usually works on John Madden's football video games.

But Delhomme called "heads." Then the official flipped the coin—and it bounced off Rucker's foot.

It came up "tails." Delhomme furiously and creatively lobbied for another coin toss—he kept trying to say that Rucker's foot caused interference—but to no avail.

The game almost ended immediately. John Kasay had to save an apparent touchdown on the kickoff, and New Orleans started at the Carolina 46. One first down and then a field goal—that was the Saints' plan.

On fourth and one from the Carolina 37, New Orleans decided to go for it. The Saints handed the ball to star running

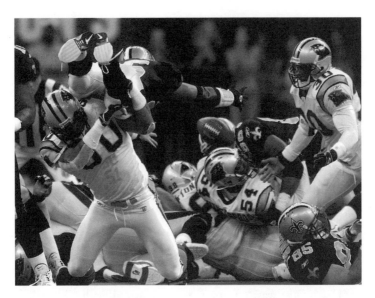

*Julius Peppers made the key play in the 2003 rematch between Carolina and New Orleans, upending Deuce McAllister on fourth down in overtime and causing a fumble. The Panthers' Kris Jenkins recovered the ball and Carolina won, 23-20. (Photo by David T. Foster III/*The Charlotte Observer*)*

back Deuce McAllister, who leaped high toward the first-down marker.

But Julius Peppers was coming the other way.

"I was just supposed to be the person who knocked a couple of people off," Peppers said. "I wasn't supposed to make the tackle. I just went straight and came through free—I was in the right place at the right time."

Peppers's crushing hit not only stopped McAllister, it also caused a fumble recovered by Kris Jenkins.

Said Jordan Gross in the midst of the Panthers' Super Bowl run three months later: "I felt like New Orleans basically had that game in the bag. And then, suddenly, we win it. If we lose that overtime game and a couple of other ones, then suddenly we aren't in the playoffs and none of this is happening."

Carolina immediately sped down the field behind Stephen Davis and kicked the game-winning field goal. Peppers's submarine play had sent the Panthers skyrocketing again.

Two Yogi-isms

That win at New Orleans also prompted one of the better Carolina Panther mixed metaphors of all time.

Said wide receiver Steve Smith after the Panthers' sixth win in seven games: "We've just got to ride this horse until the wheels come off."

That sentence reminded me of one of my favorite all-time Panther player quotes. I'm not going to name the player here, because he just wasn't a smart guy no matter how hard he tried. I don't want to unnecessarily embarrass him.

I asked him once in the Panthers locker room to describe how best to play his position.

"Well," he said, "you sure don't need to be a rocket surgeon to play it."

As you can imagine, this guy was neither rocket scientist nor brain surgeon, but his mixture of the two clichés was a classic.

The 10-Year Anniversary

The road win against New Orleans on October 26, 2003, also marked a significant anniversary. It had been exactly 10 years ago that Panthers owner Jerry Richardson—the only current NFL owner to also have played in the league—was awarded the NFL's 29th franchise.

"We spent six years trying to get the franchise," Richardson recalled happily that day from the visiting owner's suite in New Orleans' Superdome. "It wasn't really the economic investment—it was the emotional and psychological investment we had made. Nobody can describe how you feel about that. I would say the ultimate fantasy for a former NFL player would be to own your own team. Then on top of that, own your own stadium and build it the way you want to build it and operate it the way you want to operate it."

A few days after Richardson was awarded the franchise in 1993, he made a bold prediction at a pep rally in Charlotte that Carolina would win a Super Bowl within 10 years. It's a statement he never would make now.

"It isn't near what I thought it would be," Richardson said that day of owning an NFL team. "I actually thought it would be easier. It's much more difficult to win—not only to have a winning season but to win a game is difficult in the National Football League.

"And as I've said before, when things are not going as well, it is really a tough situation to be in. When things aren't going right, it seems like an eternity."

A Fearsome Foursome

A trend had developed by the time the Panthers entered the second half of the 2003 season. Every opposing coach and every broadcaster would praise their front four to the high heavens. It was becoming stylish to call the group—left defensive end Julius Peppers, left tackle Brentson Buckner, right tackle Kris Jenkins and right end Mike Rucker—"the best front four in the NFL."

For further description of the final four, consult safety Mike Minter.

"Buckner would definitely be the coach," Minter said. "Rucker is the blue-collar player. Jenkins is the power. Peppers is the athletic one, the finesse guy. Put it all together, and they're something else."

Buckner's Memory

A t 310 pounds, Brentson Buckner wasn't even the biggest defensive tackle on the team. Kris Jenkins was 335 (and sometimes more—he gets up to 350 if he's not careful about what he eats).

But Buckner still retained a vivid memory of when he tried to play football in the sixth grade. As a 175-pound sixth grader growing up in Georgia, Buckner was deemed too big for the league.

"The first time I went to play I was too heavy and I cried because all my friends were playing," Buckner said. "I'll never forget that day—me and my father sitting out in the front yard. He was trying to talk to me. A guy pulled up in the car and he was a friend of my Dad. He talked to me and he told me one day people will regret this because one day I'll be paid to play football."

Rucker's Mission

M ike Rucker has this thing about his hometown. Carolina's leading sacker for 2003 talks about St. Joseph, Missouri, so often that he has imprinted some details about the city (population 102,000) into his fellow teammates' brains.

"In the locker room, a lot of guys are from big cities," Rucker said. "Miami. New York. So I always tell them about St. Joseph. I tell them that is where the Pony Express started, and it's also the home of Jesse James. I catch some flak for talking about it, but I can guarantee you ask anybody and they know where I'm from now."

Rucker isn't making the facts up, either. The Pony Express did start there. And outlaw Jesse James tried to settle down in St. Joseph and live under an assumed name. James managed to do that for awhile before—as legend has it—the outlaw was eventually shot and killed for reward money while straightening a picture in his own home.

Peppers's Preparation

A h, to be young. The Carolina Panthers' Julius Peppers is famous among his teammates for his pregame routine—or rather, the lack of one.

Said Kevin Donnalley after teaming with Peppers in the 2002 and 2003 seasons: "Peppers would sometimes show up so late on Sundays that I'd be wondering, 'Did he get hurt this week and he's inactive?'

"And it's not late like an unfocused sort of late," Donnalley continued. "It's just the fact that he's so young and so healthy, he could literally just put a uniform on and go play. I needed two hours. I needed to get lubed up, get my knees warmed up, do all the things I need to do to step on the field. Peppers? He's just like, 'Where's my helmet?'"

Drive of the Season

F or most of the first half of the 2003 season, Jake Delhomme was thought of mostly as the guy who handed the ball off to Stephen Davis. The Jacksonville win when Delhomme threw three touchdown passes was still appreciated, but was almost considered an anomaly. During Carolina's 5-0 start, Delhomme didn't throw for as many as 200 yards a single time.

But all that changed in a home game against Tampa Bay on November 9, 2003—one of the Panthers' signature victories of a magical season.

It was an up-and-down day for Delhomme against the defending world champs until the final drive. Stephen Davis wasn't playing due to injury, which meant the game was really on Delhomme's shoulders from the beginning for the first time all season.

Delhomme threw two key interceptions in the game. One of them was returned for a touchdown after Delhomme made what coach John Fox would later call "a bonehead decision."

Delhomme had also found Ricky Proehl on a 66-yard touchdown pass in the third quarter—a play that the quarterback would say later was eerily similar to the 85-yard touchdown pass Muhsin Muhammad snared in the Super Bowl.

"On both plays, Ricky and Moose just kept running and they got lost," Delhomme said.

But a 20-7 Carolina lead turned into 21-20 deficit after two Tampa Bay touchdowns.

Then Delhomme tried to throw a ball out of bounds to avoid a sack with 4:23 left, didn't get enough on it, and had that wobbler get intercepted, too.

When Delhomme returned to the sidelines after what he would later call "a terrible, terrible play," his teammates froze him out with the most brutal silent treatment they would give him in the entire 2003 season.

No one approached him. No one consoled him. No one said a thing to him.

"Hey, I wouldn't have wanted to talk to me, either," Delhomme said.

Delhomme got one more chance, down 24-20, with 2:41 left, no timeouts and the ball on the Carolina 22.

And then came a sweet awakening for a Carolina team that had lost two of its previous three games.

Delhomme led the team in a full sprint down the field, completing five passes to five different receivers. Among them: a dart up the middle to Proehl for 29 yards, a rainbow floater to Muhammad for 22 and the touchdown pass to a slanting Smith for the final five yards and a 27-24 win. Smith would flex his muscles and scream in celebration.

In Delhomme's words right after the game, the drive went like this: "First play I hit [Kris] Mangum over the middle for a first down. The next play, I threw short to Ricky Proehl on the right. He had a big hole—I just couldn't get enough on it to get it there to him. We came right back with Karl Hankton over the middle. And then Ricky down the seam [for 29 yards].

"It seemed like they were giving us some things down the field today. Obviously they didn't respect us throwing it down the field.... When they went to one high safety, I saw the matchup and kind of knew I wanted to go there. I got hit when I threw it, so I never saw the play. I know Moose made a great catch [for 22 yards] from the crowd.

And then we thought about clocking it on that last play, but when you're going like that, you just want to go! We had a lot of time left [1:11], we had a first down inside the five and it was another of our two-minute plays.

"When we called it, I kind of had an idea where I wanted to go. I saw one on one with Smitty, and I trusted him to win and he did. He made a great catch."

After the TV broadcast of the game ended, Fox-TV analyst Cris Collinsworth was waiting for an elevator in the press box. Collinsworth was still stunned by what he had just seen.

"Jake Delhomme against the world champs," Collinsworth said, shaking his head in disbelief. "And he leads them down the field with no timeouts. Good Lord."

Payback Touchdown

There was no TD more fitting in 2003 than the one Stephen Davis scored against Washington in the final minute of the game to cinch Carolina's 20-17 win over the Redskins.

It was a third-effort, three-yard plunge. Davis stuck the ball over the goal line and had it batted away a fraction of a second later. The TD was originally called on the field, then survived a video review.

*Did Stephen Davis score on this play or didn't he? The officials ruled that he did, and the touchdown was the game winner in Carolina's 20-17 victory over Washington on November 16, 2003. (Photo by Patrick Schneider/*The Charlotte Observer*)*

All week long, Davis had refused to say anything bad about the Redskins. Coach Steve Spurrier had released Davis before the 2003 season and there had been rumblings out of Washington that Davis had been past his prime.

But after the TD, Davis let there be no doubt that the TD was special.

"It was personal," Davis said. "I spent seven years of my career there, and I know a lot of people there. It was very personal."

In fact, it turned out to be Spurrier who was past his prime in the NFL. Before the 2004 season ever began, Spurrier was gone in Washington, replaced by Joe Gibbs—a coach who shared John Fox's run-first philosophy and someone who would have loved to have Davis on his roster.

A Spurrier Story

Panthers center Jeff Mitchell knew very well what Washington's locker room would be like after the Panthers squeaked out that last-second win. He had experienced it at Florida, where he played center for several of Steve Spurrier's best Florida Gator teams.

"He could not handle losing," Mitchell said. "When we lost, he absolutely *lost it.* He wouldn't scream, but with his criticism he'd start to get very, very personal with both players and coaches."

Mitchell also said that although Spurrier has always been known as an offensive coach, he had "absolutely no respect" for what the offensive line actually did.

"Every time he drew a play, he'd put up huge 'X, Y and Z' letters," Mitchell said. "Those were the receivers, and that's what he cared about, where they were going. Then he'd put these five tiny dots in the middle. Those were the offensive linemen."

Moving Laterally

The most hilarious play of the Carolina Panthers season was also one of the most meaningless. But man, was it ever fun.

Trailing 25-16 and down to their final offensive snap against Philadelphia on November 30, 2003, Carolina needed a nine-point play.

Impossible, right?

Right. But not for lack of trying.

If you saw it, you will always remember it as the "lateral play." It was Carolina's answer to the 1982 Stanford-California game, which ended with a touchdown and a run through the band.

There was no band here. But there were eight laterals (compared to only five in the Stanford-California game).

"I still consider this play one of my favorite ones of the season," quarterback Jake Delhomme said months later. "It just showed me how this team never gives up, no matter how bad it looks."

The play took 45 seconds of real time—about 10 times longer than the average NFL play. Delhomme touched the ball three times—first on the initial pass to Nick Goings and then on two more crossfield laterals.

The coolest thing about it was that three offensive linemen actually got to handle the ball. Rookie Jordan Gross looked pretty athletic, tackle Todd Steussie looked decent, and guard Kevin Donnalley just looked tired.

In fact, the play lasts so long that on film you can see Donnalley grabbing his knees and sucking air. Then Donnalley has to pop up again, because Gross is throwing the ball to him.

Goings ultimately scored a 69-yard touchdown on the play, but it was called back because at least one of the laterals was obviously forward.

Trash Talking

You wouldn't guess that defensive end Mike Rucker was the Panthers' biggest on-field trash talker. Rucker is extremely polite off the field. Active in the community. Proud of his college degree from Nebraska.

And, to top it off, he doesn't curse. Neither Rucker nor Panthers safety Mike Minter curse. Teammates will back this up. They've never heard either of them say worse than "shoot."

Yet on the field, Rucker is incessant. ESPN miked him up for the Carolina-Atlanta game on December 7, 2003, and gave a national audience a taste of his jabbering.

Rucker has been known to tease an opponent for being bowlegged, to taunt them by saying, "All day—you won't ever stop me," or to tease them by screaming, "Are you scared? Better call the po-lice!"

Once, as Kris Jenkins is fond of pointing out, Rucker actually had to be removed from a game for hyperventilating because of the combination of adrenaline and constant talking.

But Rucker does have certain ground rules.

"I won't talk about anybody's mama," he said. "That's disrespectful."

The miked-up game provided a live test for Rucker's "no-cursing" edict, because in that game he badly injured his knee. Sure enough, while on his back in obvious pain, Rucker just kept saying, "Shoot! Shoot!"

Rucker said he decided to quit cursing back during his junior year at Nebraska.

"What happened? I heard myself on somebody's answering machine," Rucker said. "It sounded so bad. And I thought 'That's not me.' You never know who's listening when you're talking. A lot of kids look up to me, and I don't want to send that message. So immediately I quit—cold turkey. I feel like it makes you feel better. There are alternative words you can use that can get your point across."

NFC South Champs

After an 8-2 start, Carolina seemed was on the verge of winning the NFC South for nearly a month. But a three-game
losing streak—to Dallas, Philadelphia and Atlanta—pushed the
Panthers to 8-5.

Players started to get nervous. The locker room felt tense,
especially after the Atlanta game. The Falcons came in with a
woeful 2-10 record, but quarterback Michael Vick returned to
the Falcons' starting lineup and rushed for 141 yards and a
touchdown in Atlanta's 20-14 overtime win.

"He had basically had no work for more than 10 weeks,"
defensive tackle Brentson Buckner remembered. "And then here
we are, this vaunted defense, and the guy just literally beats us
one-handed. By himself. He's the toughest player we've ever
faced since I've been here."

The Panthers went to Arizona with another chance to
clinch the division, but the lowly Cardinals took a 14-10 lead in
the fourth quarter.

But quarterback Jake Delhomme led Carolina to 10
fourth-quarter points to eke out a 20-17 win. The final three
came on a 49-yard field goal by John Kasay, the last remaining
original Panther. Kasay was mobbed by happy teammates after
the kick with 0:04 left on the clock.

Said Buckner after Kasay's field goal: "You don't want to
go into the playoffs with doubt or on a stagger. You want to go
in there with a swagger."

With the pressure finally off, Carolina did. The Panthers
also won their last two games of the regular season, against
Detroit and the New York Giants, to finish 11-5.

Their first playoff game in seven years—a wild-card home
date against Dallas—loomed.

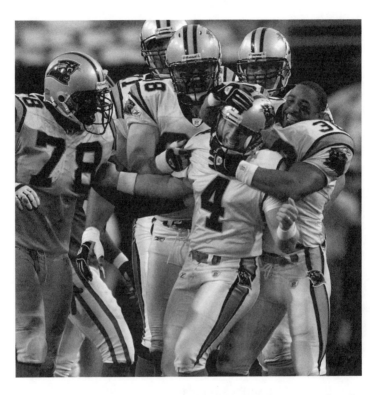

*Panthers kicker John Kasay is mobbed by his teammates after his game-winning, 49-yard field goal against Arizona on December 14, 2003. The win clinched the NFC South Division for Carolina. (Photo by Jeff Siner/*The Charlotte Observer*)*

Chapter 4

John Fox—It Is What It Is

The Carolina Panthers' run to the Super Bowl was shepherded by head coach John Fox, who took over a 1-15 team in early 2002 and pushed it into football's ultimate game only two years later.

Fox has a simple football philosophy, but the coach is a complex person. He grew up in Virginia Beach and San Diego, the son of a Navy Seal who was often gone on assignment for months at a time (much like football coaches in the midst of an NFL season). Fox was a fine surfer as a teenager and still occasionally gets on a surfboard today.

In philosophy and personality, Fox is far more similar to the Panthers' original coach, Dom Capers, than to their second coach, George Seifert.

Seifert was an aloof coach who kept his distance from everyone and everything—even the game itself. He didn't wear headphones on the sidelines because it interfered with what he called "the feel" of the game. Seifert loved to throw the ball and relished a pretty win.

Fox is an earthy storyteller who is hard to get off the phone and makes frequent rounds through the Panthers' locker room, asking about players' kids and wives. He wears sideline head-phones. He loves to run the ball and relishes a boring win. One of the first things he said in our first extended interview after he got hired in 2002 has always stuck with me: "A punt is not a bad play," he said.

Capers was a lot like that. Conservative. Well liked. Defensive-minded. Both Capers and Fox were career assistants given their first head-coaching opportunity by Panthers owner Jerry Richardson.

Fox wasn't exactly greeted with a parade in Charlotte—it was more like a shrug or a sneer. Most fans had wanted the Panthers to hire Steve Spurrier, who had just quit his job as the head coach at Florida and ended up signing on with the Washington Redskins. Fox, the gruff and garrulous defensive coordinator, was "John Who?"

In New York, though, he was well known in football cir-cles. Fox came from the New York Giants, where he was defen-sive coordinator from 1997-2001, including one season when the Giants reached the Super Bowl before losing to Baltimore. He preached there what he preaches at Carolina—that he wants "smart, tough" football players who buy into the team concept and don't commit dumb penalties.

In Fox's first season, Carolina improved from 1-15 to 7-9. In his second, the Panthers reached the Super Bowl. Yet Fox holds no illusions that those two years guaranteed his future in coaching.

"This is a production business," Fox said when we talked at length in March 2004 in an interview for this book. "If I stop producing, I'll get fired here, just like players do. The careers of players and coaches parallel each other more than most people realize."

The Panthers don't expect Fox to stop producing, though. In June 2004, they gave Fox a three-year contract extension, signing him through the 2008 season at a new salary of around $3 million per season. "John is the right fit for us," said Mark Richardson, the Panthers' team president.

Teaming with general manager Marty Hurney, a close friend, Fox has found a formula that has worked in Carolina. His players have to buy into the formula, of course. And that's what Fox was working on during his very first team meeting with the Panthers in early 2002, shortly after he was hired.

It's a meeting that has already attained legendary status in Panthers history.

The First Meeting

John Fox surveyed the room in early 2002, and he didn't much like what he saw.

These were his players now. He had just been hired as the coach of the Carolina Panthers, who had just suffered through a 1-15 season that had gotten George Seifert and his coaching staff fired.

Fox had seen some film on his team. He knew there was some talent. But he didn't think there was nearly enough toughness.

So he gave them an early taste of his coaching style. Fox recalled that meeting in detail for the first time for this book. In his own words, here is how he remembers it.

Said Fox: "You could feel the scars of those 15 straight losses in that room. And I'm just not convinced anybody in the NFL is capable of losing 15 straight games. I use the term 'laying down your sword.' Once you lay down your sword, you've got no chance. I thought that's what had happened.

"So I started off like this: 'Hey, look guys. They fired the coaches. In case you haven't figured this out, the next to go is you. I'm not threatening you. That's just the way it works in the NFL. Because George Seifert didn't drop that pass on third and 16. George Seifert didn't throw that interception. George Seifert didn't miss the tackle.'

"It ain't just the coach, not by a long shot. And if you think that's what I think, then you've got another think coming.'

*In his first ever team meeting with the Panthers after taking over for the fired George Seifert, Fox exhibited the loud voice and strong opinions his players would quickly become accustomed to. "I started off like this," Fox remembers: "Hey, look guys. They fired the coaches. In case you haven't figured this out, the next to go is you." (Photo by Patrick Schneider/*The Charlotte Observer*)*

Continued Fox: "What I wanted them to understand is that their signature was on the 1-15 season, too, not just the coaches. Hey, if I lose 15 straight here, I'll get fired, too. We all know that. And I told them that basically it was going to take a lot of hard work. I was going to see how mentally tough they were, because we needed mentally tough individuals to pull out of something like that."

The players sat there, absorbing Fox's words in silence.

Said Brentson Buckner later: "When the first thing your head coach does is question your manhood, that stings."

But Fox's tough love worked. He carried 20 players over with him from that 1-15 team to the Super Bowl squad two years later.

Said Mike Minter: "That first day he told us is that he didn't know how tough we were. He said that he knew we had talent, but mentally, I don't know how tough you are, and that he wasn't going to listen to us because we lost 15 games in a row. But if we listened to him, we would become champions. I believed him."

A Similar Speech

John Fox had actually honed that speech five years before, when he gave a very similar version to the New York Giants defense.

Fox took over as the Giants defensive coordinator in 1997. The team had gone 6-10 the season before. That New York defense had ranked 14th in the NFL and included current and future stars like Michael Strahan, Keith Hamilton and Jason Sehorn. The Giants offense had been a miserable 30th.

"We thought the offense was basically our problem," recalled Jessie Armstead, who was a Giant then and joined the Panthers to play under Fox again in early 2004. "But we had another think coming."

As Armstead remembers it, Fox started off his fiery speech like this: "You guys don't know football. And I thought, 'What are you talking about?' And then it got worse."

Fox said he also told the Giants players this: "It takes special people to have special seasons. Anybody can go through the motions. To be better than average, you have to commit more than average. Some people spend. They don't invest. You need to invest—time, effort, preparation. Invest it and you will get returns here. And what do you want to be known for anyway? Being middle of the road defensively? You're better than that!"

Armstead would make the Pro Bowl under Fox for five straight seasons. And as he says now: "We thought we knew football. But we didn't. All the packages, all the blitzes, all the stuff he brought to us—we didn't know football like he wanted us to."

It Is What It Is

John Fox is known among all the players he has coached for his reliance on clichés. Some he has picked up over the years. Some he makes up himself.

Said Panthers center Jeff Mitchell during the week of the Super Bowl about "Fox-isms": "There are a million of them. 'Don't be afraid to be great.' He always throws that one out when he is making us do something we don't want to do.... I think he has a book at home six inches thick and he references it every five years because he uses the same ones over and over. We all compare it to lobbing grenades because when you are in the locker room, he is walking away and you think the conversation is over, then he lobs a cliché at you from about 50 yards."

Fox's most famous cliché is a five-word sentence that he utters at least a dozen times a day: "It is what it is." His players unconsciously pick this one up and say it to each other. It basically means exactly what it sounds like—that you could wish life was different, but it isn't, so keep doing what you're supposed to because this is what you're stuck with. How did Fox come up with that one?

"I can't honestly tell you," Fox said. "When you're a coach, you do spend a lot of time talking. And you know sometimes players complain. They do have very hard jobs. People see the glamour of Sundays. They don't see all the work. These guys earn their money. They have to do the same things over and over again to keep their skills honed—weightlifting, practicing, all that—and it can become fairly monotonous.

"So maybe they'd come in and say, 'I'm sore,'" Fox continued. "And I'd say, 'Hey, *it is what it is.* You're sore, but you've still got to do the freakin' work.' It's just a phrase that cropped up. I got tired of saying, 'We gotta do it anyway.' I started saying, 'It is what it is,' and I guess I've never stopped."

Learning to Motivate

Fox grew up in Virginia Beach and San Diego because those were the two places his father Ron was stationed as a Navy Seal. Ron Fox did three tours of Vietnam and commanded men in the field. Fox's mother, Kaye, ran the household when her husband was gone, much like Fox's wife, Robin, does when her husband is gone now.

Ron Fox is actually Fox's stepfather, but John Fox just refers to him as his father because "he did everything for me that a father is supposed to do." John Fox has had brief contact with his biological father, but it came only after he had grown up and it isn't an ongoing relationship.

As a kid, John Fox would sometimes go down to the military base to watch his father in action.

"There are really some strong correlations between what he did and what I do now," Fox said. "You're teaching men how to do something that's potentially harmful to them. There's a lot of pressure, a lot of fear. Going into battle is very similar—and I'm not making light of battle, that's the ultimate, and much more important than football. But there are some similarities between football and battle."

The Surfer Dude

It may be hard to imagine John Fox as a "Beach Boys" type of character, surfing for hours in California. But it used to happen quite frequently.

Growing up on both the East and West coasts, Fox had learned to surf by the time he was 10. By the time he was a teenager, he was pretty good at it. And by the time he was college age and able to travel, he spent some time traveling all over the world looking for the best waves.

"Australia, New Zealand, Tahiti—I've surfed in every one of those places," Fox said. "I've been all over Mexico. San Diego has some great breaks. I've been all over Hawaii. That was mostly right after college, when I had time to travel. But I can still do it. The last time I got on a board was in 2003 in San Diego. My best friend has a sort of timeshare in Fiji, where there are some of the top breaks in the world. It's a long plane flight, though. With four kids, we haven't been able to make it out there yet."

"Crash" Fox

The Panthers' coach loved to play football, but he wasn't good enough to make it to the NFL. "My goal in life from a very young age was to play football as long as I could and then to become a coach," John Fox said.

In California during his senior year in high school, Fox broke his collarbone and missed the entire football season except for one game. Because of that, any potential scholarship disappeared. So Fox went to junior college for two years and then transferred to San Diego State, where he walked on and earned a scholarship as a hard-hitting defensive back who loved to stick his helmet into a pile.

"I finally earned a starting job and then broke my collarbone again in about the third game," Fox said.

Fox did letter twice at San Diego State in the mid-1970s and also started his coaching career there in 1978 as a graduate assistant. As a safety at San Diego State, he played alongside a gifted cornerback named Herman Edwards, who would later also become an NFL head coach. Edwards still remembers Fox's nickname as a player: "Crash."

A Father/Son Relationship

In his early years as an assistant coach, John Fox moved almost every year. At one point, he held eight different coaching jobs in an eight-year span in places as diverse as Boise, Idaho, Lawrence, Kansas, and Los Angeles.

As he learned more about players, he found his coaching style. It's tough but fair, laced with both caring and discipline.

Fox and his wife, Robin, have four kids of their own— three boys and a girl. Fox tries to treat his players like his own children, and he has explained it to them in that way for years. He did the same thing in Charlotte.

"A lot of our players have children of their own now," Fox said. "Doing what I do is a lot like being a parent. You've got to have discipline. There are things I'm going to make them do that they don't want to do. But I'm the caretaker of the organization. They're young people. They need direction, although they've done something right to get this far."

Fox said he believes the fact that a lot of the players in an NFL locker room are rich doesn't make his life—or theirs—any simpler.

"Most people think the minute you get money it helps you deal with life, that it makes life easier," Fox said. "In reality, the more money you get, the more complicated the life becomes. Some guys aren't equipped for it. As a coach, you deal with so much more than Xs and Os. Especially as a head coach, a very small percentage is Xs and Os."

Taking His Time

Why is John Fox a good coach? Sure, he knows defense and he understands how to occasionally root out a bargain like Jake Delhomme. But here's one of the more intangible reasons.

Said Stephen Davis: "Every time coach Fox sees my son, he always talks to him and plays with him. A lot of coaches aren't like that."

Game Balls All Around

John Fox's first season as the Panthers' head coach, in 2002, began with a bang. Carolina won its first three games in a row—a startling start for a team that had gone 1-15 only one year ago.

Then the roof fell in. The Panthers still had a number of holes on both offense and defense, and they started losing. One game. Two. Four. Eight straight.

Among them was a stunner at Dallas, when Carolina dominated the whole way and led 13-0 in the fourth quarter before giving up two touchdowns. The first one should have been an interception, but the ball bounced off Deon Grant's hands into Joey Galloway's arms for an 80-yard touchdown.

That loss still hurts Fox. Like many coaches, he is more prone to remember losses than wins. The Panthers also got embarrassed twice during the streak by Atlanta teams led by traditional Panthers nemesis Michael Vick—30-0 and 41-0.

So when Carolina finally won again on December 1, 2002—13-6 on the road, against a good Cleveland team that would make the playoffs that season—Fox decided it was time for everyone to get a game ball.

Not just players and coaches. Equipment men. Trainers. The radio guys. Every single person who had made the trip on the team plane.

"Even now," said Panthers play-by-play man Bill Rosinski, "that game ball means so much to me."

Said Fox: "I did it because we had lost eight games in a row. We had had some off-field issues. Cleveland was a team that was in the playoff hunt. We were a warm-weather team going to a cold-weather place. I just thought it was a huge win for us at that point in time. I thought that win kind of catapulted us, really. People had kept working hard when things didn't look so good from outside in. We never lost hope. So the game-ball thing was just rewarding people who had worked very, very hard."

A '7-11' Schedule

The Panthers' first coach, Dom Capers, usually spent three nights a week on a fold-out couch in his office in the bowels of the stadium. But John Fox has never been a believer in spending all night at work.

"From Monday through Thursday every week during the season, our coaches are basically here at 7 a.m. and go home around 11 p.m.," Fox said. "That's a lot of hours. That's plenty.

*Carolina defensive tackle Brentson Buckner dumps a bucket of ice water on Panthers coach John Fox in the closing seconds of the Panthers' NFC Championship win over Philadelphia on January 18, 2004. Fox inherited a 1-15 team and in two years got the Panthers to the Super Bowl. (Photo by Christopher A. Record/*The Charlotte Observer*)*

I always tell guys that if you're not getting it done between 7 and 11, something's wrong."

That schedule means that Fox barely sees his kids during the season, which is why he's so appreciative of his wife, Robin. "I get a glimpse of my kids early in the morning, since school starts pretty early around here, but that's about it until Friday," Fox said.

Air Bags Everywhere

John Fox's oldest son began learning how to drive in 2003. The coach did manage to find time to instruct his son on the finer points of that important skill.

"I basically taught him," Fox said. "But let me tell you, it scares the heck out of me."

At Christmas 2003, Fox got his son an Infiniti with four-wheel drive. "It's big enough to be safe, and there are air bags all over the thing," Fox said. "That's what I wanted to know—just how many air bags it had."

The Bear Hug

When it's time for business with John Fox, it's time for business. You hardly ever see him smile on the sidelines. He mostly chomps gum, shouts orders and looks intense. He is constantly searching players' eyes, trying to see how hungry they still are and how much they have left on that particular Sunday.

Although the players enjoy Fox's sense of humor, they don't see it much when it's time to put in the game plan. When Fox is addressing the entire team, he doesn't make many jokes. It's straight ahead—This is what we need to do. This is what we can't do.

That sort of "stern professor" image made what happened late in the 2003 season even funnier to everyone who witnessed it.

Rod "He Hate Me" Smart, the Panthers' eccentric special-teamer, always sat directly in front of Fox in the team auditorium. Smart liked the front row. The team was deep into the season, trying to find a way to get motivated before another long week of preparation for the next game.

Suddenly, just before Fox was about to turn on the overhead and start talking about opponents' tendencies, Smart grabbed Fox and gave him a hug.

A bear hug.

A long, long bear hug.

Said offensive guard Kevin Donnalley: "He hugged Fox like a little kid hugging his dad. Head on his shoulder. The whole bit. Fox is looking around, his arms are straight out—he didn't know what to do. It was one of the funniest things I've ever seen in my life."

Said Fox: "It was so out of the blue, and people just started cracking up. That's the thing about Rod. He's unique. But he's got a great passion for football. And every team needs some people who are going to make you laugh."

Just Chopping Wood

Among John Fox's favorite clichés is to "keep chopping wood."

That one is fairly common in the NFL. Like most of the clichés that coaches use, it basically means to keep working hard. "Keep chopping wood and the tree will fall," Donnalley remembered. "Coach Fox was always using that one."

Fox's defensive coordinator, Jack Del Rio, was also prone to using the phrase in 2002. And the Panthers' defense chopped a lot of wood that season, improving from No. 31 to No. 2 in the entire NFL in total defense.

By virtue of that performance, Del Rio got the head-coaching job in Jacksonville in 2003. And he brought a lot of Carolina with him, including the "chopping wood" cliché.

But Del Rio took the cliché a step further than Fox ever had. The coach had a tree stump with an axe placed in the Jaguars' locker room in September 2003. Players were welcome to pick up the axe and take a swing at the stump whenever they wanted to.

On October 9, 2003, Jacksonville punter Chris Hanson picked up the axe and swung it. The axe blade ricocheted off the stump and directly into Hanson's right shin.

That was it for Hanson that season—he would miss the rest of the year. It took a four-hour surgery to put his leg back together.

Said Del Rio after the incident: "I think that it's safe to say I'll find another slogan."

And since Hanson's accident, whether it's coincidence or not, you hardly ever hear Fox talk about "chopping wood" anymore.

Chapter 5

Doomsday for Dallas

When the TV schedule was announced for wild-card weekend, the Carolina Panthers drew the best spot. They would host the Dallas Cowboys on Saturday, January 3, 2004 at 8 p.m.

That wasn't due to the Panthers' national appeal, of course. The Cowboys, long known as "America's Team," were responsible for the prime-time slot. They had the star on their helmets, coach Bill Parcells on their sideline and one win over Carolina already during the season—a 24-20 win in Texas.

The Panthers felt they had been too cautious defensively in that game, letting Dallas quarterback Quincy Carter become too comfortable in the pocket. Carter had thrown 44 times in the game, completing 29 and keeping Carolina off-balance.

Panthers coach John Fox believed 20 points would win this game. Dallas had the NFL's No. 1 defense, but Carolina was rounding into form with the return of linebacker Dan Morgan.

It was a balmy January night in Charlotte—63 degrees at kickoff. A frenzied crowd of 72,324 fans showed up, wearing shirtsleeves and swinging towels provided at the gate.

And Carolina played a nearly perfect game. The Panthers committed no turnovers and had no penalties, whipping Dallas

*Mike Rucker was part of the Panthers' near-perfect performance against Dallas in the 2003 playoffs. The Panthers had no turnovers and committed no penalties in their 29-10 win. (Photo by Christopher A. Record/*The Charlotte Observer*)*

29-10. This chapter provides a behind-the-scenes look at some of the best moments of Carolina's first playoff appearance in seven years.

The Speech

Before every game, coach John Fox picks one player or coach to give a speech to motivate the team. He doesn't announce who it is beforehand, so it's always a surprise to the players.

This time, it was Sam Mills.

Mills had been fighting cancer since he was diagnosed in August. Since he had returned to work, the players had been so fearful of impinging on Mills's privacy that hardly anyone had asked him about it. Cancer was the elephant in the room when Mills was there—everyone knew he had it, but no one talked about it.

"I really would have told them whatever they wanted to know, because people do need to be educated," Mills said. "But most guys were so respectful of my privacy they really didn't ask much. So the speech before the Dallas game was the first time I really told them in much detail what was wrong with me."

Mills told the players to never give up on the field, even if they thought they were beaten on a particular play.

"When I found out I had cancer, there were two things I could do—quit or keep pounding," Mills said. "I'm a fighter. I kept pounding. You're fighters, too. Keep pounding."

Many players would later point to that speech as the most inspirational one they had heard in their Panthers career.

The First Pass

After Dallas punted on its first possession, Carolina got the ball and ran Stephen Davis up the middle twice. Normal stuff. The Panthers' first pass play wasn't unusual either—on third and three, Jake Delhomme dropped back and looked for Steve Smith on about a seven-yard out route that was simply designed to get the first down.

"But I saw what the corner was doing and I cut it inside," Smith said.

After catching the ball, Smith began what would be a sparkling postseason by darting right past Dallas cornerback Terence Newman. Safety Roy Williams came over to help Newman, but he was way too slow.

Suddenly, Smith was off. He sprinted down the sideline, only to get knocked off his feet at the 1-yard line by Dallas cornerback Pete Hunter.

"Oh, my friends were on me for that," Smith said. "They were like, 'You're supposed to be fast!' They had fun with it. And when you watch the film, of course the other receivers were all over me. 'How did you ever get caught?'"

In reality, though, Smith's 70-yard gain set the tone for the game. It led to a Carolina field goal and helped ensure that the Panthers never trailed.

The First Touchdown

With Carolina clinging to a 6-0 lead and holding the ball at the Dallas 23 in the second quarter, Jake Delhomme called timeout. It was then that the game turned permanently in Carolina's favor.

On the sideline, the Panthers decided to go with a draw play on third and 10. Delhomme handed the ball to Stephen Davis. The line blocked it perfectly. Suddenly, Davis was side-stepping into the end zone for the game's first touchdown.

That made it 13-0. But once the play ended, Panther Jeff Mitchell thought it was pretty much over.

"In that first game when we played them and we lost, I felt like we were tired and they manhandled us up front," Mitchell said. "It was our worst game of the year as an offensive line. It felt like they had 13 guys out there. That was a whipping.

"But this time," Mitchell continued, "the biggest factor in that game was I think Dallas was tired. I think they were beaten down and kind of wanting to go home, to be honest with you. Maybe with Bill Parcells chewing on you every week, that may make you want you to go home. I don't know. But once we got up on them with that touchdown, honestly? They were done."

The Linebacker

Panthers middle linebacker Dan Morgan provided a preview against Dallas of the way he would play throughout the playoffs. Morgan was everywhere—flowing to the ball on the run, blitzing or guarding a running back on the pass.

Morgan, Panthers linebackers coach Sam Mills believes, could be one of the best to ever play the game—if Morgan can stay healthy. Mills doesn't hand out large praise lightly, but he really thinks Morgan could be hall of fame material if he could string together a bunch of seasons at the same level of play he had in the final month of the 2003 season.

Morgan would agree.

"I've had a lot of frustration," Morgan said. "A lot of injuries. A lot of negative comments. But I know that when I'm healthy, I'm one of the best linebackers in the NFL."

For the first time in his NFL career, on December 15, 2003, Morgan wore a mouthpiece against Detroit. He hoped that would help prevent another concussion—he had trouble with those earlier in the season.

And it worked. Morgan wore the mouthpiece throughout the playoffs as well.

Said Mills: "We're a different defense with Dan Morgan on the field. He's fast, he's instinctive, he's got a good change of direction and his mentality is that he's going to make every play. He's hard to block because he's always thinking he's going to get there. It's hard to deny him."

Mills, a former five-time Pro Bowl linebacker himself, said that it's surprisingly easy in the NFL to find defenders ready to give up after they get blocked.

"Some guys—their thinking just stops them from making a play," Mills said. "It's like, 'Oh, here's my block. They got me this time.' But hey, they are going to have a block for you. Your job is to get free."

With Morgan healthy throughout the Dallas game, Carolina could play Will Witherspoon in his more natural outside linebacker position. The Panthers don't like sticking Witherspoon in the middle, where he's a bit undersized.

"The thing about Dan being healthy, too, is it affects Will Witherspoon," Mills said. "He prepares all week to play one position and then he plays another in the game if Dan is hurt. And Will's not built for the middle. He's just a smart kid, and tough enough and willing enough to do it."

The Rest of the Game

The Panthers never did let Dallas have a chance that night. John Kasay would end up kicking five field goals for Carolina, and the defense held the Cowboys to only 10 points. Julius Peppers had a late interception to cement the game and got a hug from coach John Fox as he came off the field, still holding the ball.

The win would set up Carolina's trip to St. Louis. The Panthers would be a longshot to win there—the Rams had won 14 straight games at home. Plus, St. Louis also was coming off a first-round playoff bye. The Rams and the Eagles were seeded No. 1 and No. 2 in the NFC playoffs and had gotten byes. Carolina, the No. 3 seed, had had to play.

But the Panthers were at least helping to solve their identity-crisis problem. The Dallas game was witnessed by a national TV audience, including regular *Monday Night Football* announcers Al Michaels and John Madden.

Michaels made an interesting point on TV, saying that he and Madden both lived on the West Coast and that many people out there had no idea in what city the "Carolina Panthers" actually play.

After this game, a few million more of them knew the right answer.

*Julius Peppers added one last dash of seasoning to the Panthers' play-off romp over Dallas, intercepting Quincy Carter late in the fourth quarter to seal the Carolina victory and earn a congratulatory hug from coach John Fox. (Photo by Christopher A. Record/*The Charlotte Observer*)*

A Girl Named Hope

All of the Carolina Panthers' lives were touched by cancer in some way in the summer of 2003, when linebacker Mark Fields and linebackers coach Sam Mills were both diagnosed with the disease in a two-week period.

But one Carolina Panther later the same year helped the story of one little girl with cancer touch the lives not only of his teammates and their fans, but also of the nation.

Offensive guard Kevin Donnalley met 12-year-old Hope Stout before a Panthers home game on October 19, 2003. The redheaded girl had a rare, aggressive type of bone cancer called osteosarcoma. The two shared a few moments together on the field. Somebody snapped a few pictures.

Donnalley had met children with illnesses before. With three kids of his own, he had a soft spot for them. But that day affected him deeply. After the game, he couldn't get Hope out of his mind.

"Something was pushing me to take the next step," Donnalley said. "Call her. Get to know her. Try to help. My belief is that God had a plan for not only the Panthers to do well this season, but for me to meet Hope and to try and help her. Our courses collided. And she was the one who actually helped me, to grow as a person and to understand the way every person should strive to be."

Hope was asked by a Make-A-Wish Foundation representative shortly after her diagnosis what she would wish for if she could have anything in the world. She turned the question around on the questioner. How many other children with life-threatening illnesses were on the regional list, needing a wish granted?

The answer was 155.

Hope, rather than wishing for something for herself, wished for those 155 dreams to be fulfilled.

It would take $1 million to do it, organizers figured.

Donnalley helped all he could. He got involved with the family—the Stouts and Donnalley both lived near each other on the south side of Charlotte. He helped out with several major fundraisers for Hope's cause. And then he got ABC TV's Lisa Guerrero interested.

Guerrero was in Charlotte to do the Panthers-Cowboys playoff game on January 3, 2004, as the sideline reporter. She broadcast the story nationwide that night and showed a picture of Donnalley and Hope together.

"After the game, I came back into the locker room," Donnalley said. "Everyone's wanting to go back out and get high-fives from our fans and I'm saying, 'Somebody just tell me now, did Hope get on the game or not?'"

Donnalley finally heard that it did.

The local Make-A-Wish organization didn't raise that $1 million it needed.

With Donnalley's help, it raised $1.6 million.

And counting.

Hope Stout died the day after the Panthers-Cowboys game, on January 4, 2004.

"Now Make-A-Wish is planning ways to do national campaigns around Hope Stout's story," Donnalley said. "With so much craziness going on, when something like this happens in the world, you want to grab onto it, you really do. I have as many people ask me what it was like to be around Hope and how can they get involved as I do about how it was to be in the Super Bowl."

To learn more about Make-A-Wish, visit the website www.wish.org.

Delhomme's Necklace

After the Dallas game, the Panthers returned to the field to circle the stadium and slap hands with their fans. It was something of a tradition—the 1996 team had done the exact same thing after beating Dallas in a playoff game. That game was the Panthers' only playoff victory in their history until this one.

Coach John Fox had been made well aware of how well the 1996 team's return to greet the fans had been received. When the Panthers won, shortly after he talked to the team in the locker room he said, "Let's get back out there!"

Off the Panthers went, jubilantly giving high-fives to every Panther fan who could get down close to field level.

"Those fans had been waiting a long, long time for something good to happen here," Brentson Buckner said. "We owed them at least that lap—probably even more."

During the "victory lap" around the stands, someone slipped a Mardi Gras-type necklace around Jake Delhomme's neck.

A picture taken shortly after that moment is shown on page 2 of this book.

"I don't even know who it was who gave me the beads, but I liked them," Delhomme said. "I wore them proudly."

Chapter 6

The World According to Steve Smith

The most controversial, explosive, exhilarating player the Carolina Panthers have ever had wears electric blue shoes on his feet, No. 89 on his back and a mountainous chip on his shoulder.

The Panthers have never suited up anyone quite like Steve Smith. Before he turned 25, Smith had already scored the most famous touchdown in Panthers history (in the playoff game against St. Louis) and beaten up a teammate in the Panthers' film room (Anthony Bright, for which Smith earned a one-game suspension).

There was much more to Smith than those two five-second bursts, of course. In an exclusive interview for this book, Smith went into unprecedented detail about his life growing up in inner-city Los Angeles and how that has affected him. He also talked about the unusual, solitary walk he takes to Bank of America Stadium before every Panther home game, as well as his well-earned reputation for bluntness and his love for helping coach his son's soccer team.

"Everybody thinks they know me," Smith said. "Nobody really has a clue who I am."

This chapter should give you that clue.

It contains a heavy dose of Steve Smith on Steve Smith, along with some of his teammates' and coaches' thoughts on this electrifying player. For better or for worse, Smith isn't going anywhere anytime soon at Carolina—he signed a six-year, $26.5-million contract extension in early 2004.

"The Best You'll Ever Get"

When Smith entered the league in 2001 as a third-round draft choice out of Utah chosen by then-Panthers coach George Seifert, his insecurity manifested itself in some of the cockiest comments you had ever heard.

"I wanted to show people I could play and I carried that around," Smith said. "Sometimes my comments reflected that. I sat down in [Panthers general manager] Marty Hurney's office in my rookie year when we were negotiating my contract. He had offered me something low. And I told him, 'Marty, I'm going to be the best player you're ever going to get here. I'm the best player you'll ever get in the draft. I don't care what other people have done. I know how good I am.'

Hurney, the Panthers' general manager, was almost speechless.

"He said something like, 'Well, I hope so,'" Smith said.

Backing It Up

Steve Smith didn't waste much time starting to make his own prediction come true. In his first ever NFL game, on September 9, 2001, he lined up to receive the opening kickoff.

*Steve Smith emerged as the Panthers' big-play threat in 2003, hauling in many passes like this 52-yard touchdown against Indianapolis. Smith foretold his destiny with the Panthers during a contract meeting his rookie year, telling the Panthers brass he would be "the best player you're ever going to get." (Photo by Patrick Schneider/*The Charlotte Observer*)*

Smith was angry at the time. That's not unusual. He frequently finds some way to work himself into a lather before games. Like tennis player John McEnroe in his glory days, Smith is one of the few pro athletes who actually plays better in a controlled rage.

Before the Super Bowl, Smith worked himself up by obsessing on all the questions that reporters had asked him during the week about how physical New England's secondary was.

In his first game ever, he latched onto something else.

Recalled Smith: "When I was warming up catching kickoffs, this Minnesota special teams player whose name I forget comes over and says, 'This ain't Utah no more, son.' And that sparked me. That was the wrong thing to say. And when I hit that hole, I hit that hole hard. I was mad. I felt like I couldn't stink that day. And he had brought me back down."

Smith wasn't down for long. He took that kickoff back 93 yards for a touchdown.

Even now, after his Super Bowl touchdown and the famous "arms-outstretched" TD to win the playoff game against St. Louis, Smith considers his opening-kickoff score against Minnesota the favorite TD of his career.

"My daughter had been induced that Tuesday afternoon," Smith said. "We had her in Charlotte on September 5, 2001. She was supposed to be born on September 11, actually. So I kept my wristband on from the hospital after her birth, and I said I wasn't going to take it off until I scored. I wore it for the kickoff. And when I scored, I got to take it off. I kept it, though. I just put it in my sock for the rest of the game."

A Lofty Goal

Steve Smith thought he would score in that first game. Most people didn't. He has set similarly high goals for himself throughout his career, and before the 2004 season he voiced his ultimate goal.

"I want to get into the Pro Football Hall of Fame," Smith said. "People may say, 'You're not good enough.' Yadda yadda yadda. And those are the people that get the blunt answer from me, too. Screw you. How you going to tell me what I can't do? I'm going to do whatever it takes."

The Walking Man

Smith has one of the stranger pregame routines in the NFL. Every NFL team is transported by bus to the stadium. That's true even for home games. Saturday nights are spent at a local hotel, so that the home team can make sure its players are focused on the game and not out carousing.

But Smith, who spent much of his early life on buses, walks to the games instead. The Panthers have stayed at two different uptown Charlotte hotels the night before home games during Smith's tenure with the team, and he has walked about 20 to 30 minutes to the stadium from each one.

Smith has always been an early riser—as a kid he would sometimes go to bed at 6:30 p.m. and get up at 4 a.m. He usually awakes on game days by 6 a.m. "By then, I have no more sleep left in me," he said.

He eats breakfast at the team hotel, talks to his wife on the phone and then packs his Reebok backpack. Inside, he carries a change of clothes and his Bible.

"For a 1 p.m. game, I usually leave around 9 or 9:30," Smith said. "I just wear jeans and a sweater or sweatshirt, and I always walk by myself.

"See," Smith continued, "back home in L.A. I used to walk all the time. The bus system was never on time. So what I'd do is walk to the next bus stop and look. If it wasn't coming, I'd walk to the next one. And I'd just keep walking until the bus came.

"Those were the walks where I used to dream of playing in the NFL. I used to dream about doing exactly what I'm doing now. So now, on each of those walks before games, my mind goes back to it. That's what I think about—how I made it here."

Scraping By

Steve Smith grew up in a rough neighborhood in Los Angeles. His mother, Florence Young, was a drug counselor for the county government. She raised him and his younger brother, Ravonn, by herself.

Said Smith: "I was kind of a Mama's boy. So I kind of hung out with mom sometimes at work. She did things on the weekend and took us. And we interacted with people who were recovering alcoholics, recovering crackheads, recovering heroin addicts—all that stuff. I was around those people because my mom thought they were good people. She wanted me to be around people who weren't afraid to admit their mistakes. Sometimes we'd play cards or dominoes with those people."

Smith said that there was a lot of gang activity where he grew up. He said he didn't join a gang, but that many of his friends and acquaintances did. Sometimes, gunshots outside prompted his mom to make him stay inside for the evening.

"There have been times in my life where I've done stuff because of how I grew up," Smith said. "You get used to doing things where you really don't care about the outcome.

"You just go with your gut instinct and whatever happens, happens."

A Weekend Father

Smith occasionally saw his father, but not often. He would sometimes stay with his father on weekends.

"He paid us a little child support," Smith said. "It wasn't much but he did it, and he did it when he felt like it. As I grew older, we really grew apart.

"It was like, 'Aww, Dad, let's go play basketball.' And he'd say, 'No, I'm tired.' I'd go over to his house and then end up just playing by myself. There were times when we did stuff. But it wasn't consistent."

Smith said that unreliable relationship has ensured his involvement with his own children be intense.

"I try to do things with them over the top," Smith said. "That's why I coach soccer. In the off season I'm there, giving the kids high-fives. I coach my son in soccer because I *want* to be out there with him."

Taco Bell

One of Steve Smith's most vivid childhood memories is of playing a basketball game in football cleats as a kid because the cleats were the only athletic shoes he had.

"People laughed at me," Smith said. "And I scratched up the floor, too."

He was always hungry for money—and sometimes food—as a kid. A job at Taco Bell helped him solve both those problems.

"Originally, I got my Taco Bell job because I needed money," Smith said. "All my mom could afford to give me is $10 a week—and that was *some* weeks. She'd give me the 10 bucks and that was supposed to last me for the week. And sometimes it would be cut down to five. I brought my lunch sometimes, but not every time, because we didn't always have lunch meat. So when I got to be a junior I said, 'I want to get me a job.'

"I got one at Taco Bell. A girl in my class told me she was quitting. I went over there and applied and they took me. I was working there as a junior up until the time I left for Utah (close to four years). And I paid for my prom that way."

A Checkered High-School Career

Steve Smith was far from an All-American in high school. "I was only OK," Smith said. "I was a running back and a free safety, never a wide receiver."

During his sophomore year, Smith's mother decided not to let him play football because his grades were dropping. During his junior year, Smith quit the team in a huff.

"There was a senior in front of me at defensive back," Smith said. "He wasn't as good as me, but he had paid his dues. Instead of just sticking it out and battling him, I quit. I decided I was just going to play basketball. Well, my basketball skills were tarnished. So I tried out and didn't even make the team. I just worked on track the whole time that year. I ran the hurdles and the 100."

Smith rejoined the football team as a senior and did start. "But my grades weren't good at all," he said. "I didn't even take the SAT. I didn't care. I never applied myself in school. I didn't want to find out that I couldn't go."

Saved by Junior College

Steve Smith did attract some attention from local junior colleges, though, because he had some good moments in high school. He decided to try one of them. And it was there, at Santa Monica Junior College, that Smith began to get his athletic and academic act together. Often riding as much as two hours on the bus to get to school and practice, Smith got switched to receiver early in his career and began to shine.

At Santa Monica, Smith also teamed with another receiver who would go on to star in the NFL—the Cincinnati Bengals' Chad Johnson. As a college sophomore, Smith scored 14 touchdowns, and that earned him a scholarship to Utah, where he would ultimately meet his wife, Angie, and play well enough to get drafted in the third round by the Panthers.

Smith probably would have been chosen higher in the 2001 NFL draft, but some teams were scared away by his 5-9 height—not realizing that Smith's jumping ability has meant he has been able to dunk a basketball since the ninth grade.

Seifert's Legacy

Some of the Panthers' players don't bother to disguise their disdain for former coach George Seifert. Steve Smith didn't mind Seifert, though.

"First of all, he was the coach that drafted me," Smith said. "Seifert told me, 'Don't screw it up' and then hardly ever talked to me again. He didn't care what you thought, he was going to do it his way. And you've got to kind of respect that a little bit."

The Coaches and Smith

Ever since John Fox took over as Panthers coach in early 2002, Steve Smith has been one of his projects. Fox was the coach who promoted Smith to starting wide receiver in 2002 and the one who began to feature Smith far more prominently in the offense in 2003. He also was the one who punished Smith with the one-game suspension after Smith hit Bright in the Panthers' film room and the one who has tried to calm Smith down at various other times.

Said Fox of his coaching style with Smith and other challenging players: "You're basically teaching them how to be men, and some guys require a little extra work. You can get mad at them and get rid of them—that's the easy thing to do. That'd be like when your kid does something stupid, you kick them out of the family.

"My relationship with Steve has been trying to just help him grow up. Sometimes, these guys need some direction. With Steve, there was talent. I explain to the guys, 'Talent is easy. You're born with it. Discipline? That's hard. The great ones have both.'"

The Panthers' offensive coordinator, Dan Henning, has grown to really like Smith. Henning said during Super Bowl week: "Steve Smith is one of the finest fathers and husbands and sons that you will ever be around. Steve Smith, like a lot of players in this league, came from nowhere. He came up from an environment where probably 75 percent of the guys he grew up with are still down and out, and maybe in jail… He has had to fight his way right through everything to get where he is. He is not hard to relate to. He is very emotional. He is very paranoid over certain things because of the way he grew up."

Bluntness

Steve Smith's reputation for saying whatever he wants to has been intact since the day he came to Carolina. "A lot of people want you to tell them what they want to hear," Smith said. "I'm just the opposite. That irritates me. Just shoot me straight. Tell me what you think, and I'll tell you if I like it or dislike it. I hate not knowing what's going on. It makes me nervous."

Said Kevin Donnalley, Smith's teammate for three years: "Steve often will say things that everybody is saying, but because of our society it would be politically incorrect. We put muzzles on everybody so you don't say the wrong thing. Usually what he says is right on. Sometimes you'll hear him speak and you'll say, 'Oh, Steve, why did you say that?' and then sometimes he'll say something right on, and you know what? That needed to be said. That needed to be out there."

Spinning the Ball

One of Steve Smith's signature moves after a big catch or punt return is the ball spin. He flicks the ball onto the ground quickly with a wrist turn, often causing it to spin like a top for several seconds.

Said Smith: "When I do that, you'll know that I'm getting into the groove. I'm not doing it to embarrass people. I'm just excited. I'm getting into that groove. There are times in the game I get three or four plays called to me back to back, and that's when I'll do it.

"What the spin says is, 'You better watch out now.' It's kind of like Michael Jordan when he used to shoot and then he'd hold that pose for a minute, and he'd turn around. He was like, 'I'm getting hot! I'm getting hot!' That's what it means."

Bin Ball

One of the games the Panthers have developed and honed for several years to kill time in the locker room is called "Bin Ball."

Bin Ball is basically a form of basketball. You use a ball of tape for the basketball and a big laundry basket for the goal.

With Kevin Donnalley as the instigator, all sorts of new rules were developed. Mostly, the offensive players are the fans and the players of the game.

"It was played in front of people's lockers so you had your own gallery built in, people were cracking on you," Donnalley said. "And we had the 'passerby rule'—that was big. If someone was just walking by the game, to get a towel or get in the shower or whatever, and he messed with your shot, that was perfectly legal. Steve Smith was a frequent passerby. He was purposely trying to irritate people."

Confirmed Smith: "Oh yeah. They hated it. I would hit it in midair, and I'd hit it hard. Wherever it lands in the locker room, that's where you have to shoot it next. And I'd say, 'OK, I'm not going to do it the next time.' And then I'd do it again."

Steve and Jake

Steve Smith and Jake Delhomme made friends quickly in the 2003 training camp, well before the two knew that Delhomme would be the starter and Smith would gain 1,110 yards that season catching his passes. They shared engaging personalities. They were both eagerly impatient on the field. And they loved to verbally challenge each other, right from the beginning.

On the first day of training camp, Smith said he could tell Delhomme looked "shaky" and decided to rub it in fast. He walked up to Delhomme after practice and said: "You are a sorry quarterback."

Delhomme, stung, told Smith that the wide receiver was the one who had looked bad (although as everyone who saw the practice knew that wasn't true).

Smith retaliated. "Hey, I'm not the one who threw nine picks today," Smith said.

*Steve Smith flexes in celebration after scoring the game-winning touchdown on a five-yard pass from Jake Delhomme to beat Tampa Bay, 27-24, on November 9, 2003. That's Delhomme, his tongue wagging, about to disrupt Smith's celebration with a bear hug. (Photo by Christopher A. Record/*The Charlotte Observer*)*

"That started it," Smith says now. "We were always joking, and it was always on point.

You started looking forward to it. I'd come out to practice and say, 'What you got for me today, white boy?' And he'd say: 'What you got for me today, black man?' Or I'd be telling him during a game, 'I'm so open. But there's no way you can throw it that far anyway.'"

Smith and Delhomme also decided to occasionally alter plays on their own on the field.

"The coaches don't play," Smith explained. "They coach you in the week. But on Sunday, that's our playground. That's our mentality. We do whatever it takes for us to win, and y'all can yell at us later. There are times I've run the wrong route and Jake still has thrown it and I've caught it. We know we're going to get cussed out for changing everything in midstream. And we're like, 'Who cares?'"

Getting Paid

Steve Smith swears that his huge new contract—signed in early 2004—won't change his style. The kid who once worked at Taco Bell to supplement the $10 a week his mother gave him now will make $26.5 million over the next six years.

"A paycheck is great," Smith said. "But that doesn't define you. You can make $100 million. But your last game, if you were terrible, that's what people remember. People remember Dwight Clark for 'The Catch,' not for how much money he made. And the ball is really a receiver's paycheck anyway. The ball shows that they are paying attention to you, that they care about you."

Chapter 7

St. Louis—Game of a Lifetime

Even now, when you talk to the Carolina Panthers about the 2003 season, one game rises above the rest.

It wasn't the Super Bowl. It wasn't the NFC Championship. It wasn't any of those seven regular-season wins by three points or less.

It was St. Louis in the divisional playoffs.

On January 10, 2004, the Panthers edged St. Louis, 29-23, before a stunned crowd at the Edward Jones Dome. The game went into double overtime—the first NFL game to do so in 17 years—before Jake Delhomme and Steve Smith connected on a 69-yard touchdown pass on third and 14 to end it in shocking fashion.

In the aftermath of the game, all sorts of things were said, many of them similar to Panthers coach John Fox's first quote of his press conference: "I've never seen a game like that."

There was also this statement: "It was fun. It was one you love being a part of."

Want to guess who said that? Smith? Delhomme? Mike Minter?

None of the above.

*Steve Smith sprints into the end zone, arms wide open, at the end of the 69-yard touchdown pass that ended Carolina's double-overtime playoff win over St. Louis on January 10, 2004. Smith said later of the pose: "It was to say, 'Wow! Look at us! Not look at me—look at us. What do you think about us now?'" (Photo by Patrick Schneider/*The Charlotte Observer*)*

That was St. Louis running back Marshall Faulk. And he lost.

But Faulk understood inherently what everyone who saw this game around the country also knew instinctively. It was extraordinary.

The Panthers—underdogs by seven points—overcame a huge homefield advantage to win. St. Louis had won 14 straight games at home. The last time St. Louis and Carolina had faced each other in St. Louis, on November 11, 2001, the Rams had destroyed Carolina, 48-14.

But this time Carolina led most of the game and even boasted a 23-12 lead with three minutes left. St. Louis then mounted a furious comeback, keyed in part by an onside kick recovery, to tie the game at 23.

In overtime, the tension was unreal. On the first four possessions of overtime, each team moved inside the other team's 40 twice without scoring. Both teams missed field goals by an eyelash.

Finally, on overtime possession No. 5, Smith and Delhomme ended it.

This chapter explores what many Panthers now call the favorite game of their careers.

A "Rocky" Movie

We will get into the specifics of the game in a second. But first, let Carolina Panther offensive guard Kevin Donnalley set the tone for that afternoon.

"No matter what," Donnalley said, "the greatest game I ever played in was that St. Louis Rams game. To me, it just felt like a *Rocky* movie. It was so overly dramatic—sloppy at times, awesome at times. It was two big heavyweights going at it. Someone would hit that killer punch, and you'd think, 'That's it, game over.' And the ref would be going, '8, 9, 10!' But then the guy gets up! You think you're down and out but then we'd get up or they would. Four or five times you'd be sitting there going, 'We won it. No, we lost it. No, we won it!'

"And then the way it ended—it wasn't like we marched all the way down there and kicked a field goal to win. It was third and 14. And all of a sudden that big right cross just lands and knocks them out for good!"

Greatest Show on Turf

St. Louis averaged 27.9 points per game in the 2003 NFL regular season, tied for No. 2 in the league, and that average grew to an astonishing 33.6 points per game at home. The Rams had had a slightly better regular season than Carolina, earning them a first-round playoff bye. While Carolina had to beat Dallas simply to earn a spot in the NFL's second round of the playoffs, St. Louis didn't have to play on the first playoff weekend.

Most of the questions posed to the Panthers before the game had to do with the Rams' speed. St. Louis officials had smartly built their team to take advantage of the artificial turf at the Edward Jones Dome. Players like Marshall Faulk, Isaac Bruce and Torry Holt were all speedsters who seemed even faster on turf.

"The last time we had been to St. Louis [in the 48-14 loss], it felt like they had had 1,000 yards of total offense against us," Carolina defensive tackle Brentson Buckner said. "This time, the pressure was off. We weren't supposed to win. We weren't really even supposed to be there. So we didn't worry about how fast they were on turf. We're pretty fast, too. We went to St. Louis ready to erase some myths—especially that one."

The Rams' home audience was thinking big thoughts. St. Louis seemed primed for another Super Bowl appearance.

The front page of the Saturday, January 10 *St. Louis Post-Dispatch* sports section showed a picture of the Vince Lombardi Trophy, awarded to the Super Bowl champion and an equation that looked ahead. "W+W+W=Lombardi" it read, in essence predicting three straight Rams wins and a Super Bowl title.

Some Early Trickery

Carolina tried to go against its own tendencies in the first quarter, hoping to shake the Rams up. On the Panthers' first series, they ran a reverse to Steve Smith, and Smith threw the ball 25 yards downfield to Muhsin Muhammad.

The pass was a strike, but Muhammad dropped it.

The Rams, taking over at their own 13, immediately sped downfield on their first series. They got to first and goal at the Carolina 7. But two running plays failed, and the Rams had third and goal from the Carolina 3.

St. Louis coach Mike Martz, who was about to have a very questionable play-calling game, made his first big mistake. Rather than throw the ball, the Rams tried to run quarterback Marc Bulger on a bootleg to the left. Bulger got stuffed.

"Oooh, boy!" Panthers play-by-play man Bill Rosinski said on the radio. "I'll take that all day."

St. Louis kicker Jeff Wilkins—who would play a huge part in the game—hit from 20 yards out, and it was 3-0 Rams.

Davis's Last Carry

The Panthers thought they could run against the Rams, and it turned out they could. Carolina would end up rushing for 216 yards.

But the workhorse wasn't the man you'd expect. Stephen Davis only carried the ball six times, and DeShaun Foster carried it 21.

Davis's last carry of the game was something else, though. With Carolina trailing 6-0 early in the second quarter, Davis took a handoff at his own 32. Behind great blocking from the offensive line and tight end Kris Mangum, Davis then embarked on his longest run of the season.

Among those chasing him was St. Louis safety Jason Sehorn, who couldn't catch Davis in what would be a foreshadowing of Sehorn's struggles against Smith on the game-winning touchdown.

With about 20 yards to go to the end zone, though, Davis began to noticeably limp. He slowed up enough to get caught at the St. Louis 4 after a 64-yard run.

Diagnosed with a strained quadricep, Davis wouldn't return to the game.

Moose Bulls for the Ball

Stephen Davis's 64-yard run did set Carolina up near the goal line, and it was there that the Panthers scored one of their most unorthodox touchdowns of the season.

On third and goal from the 5, the Panthers tried an option play, with Jake Delhomme pitching the ball to DeShaun Foster. But the St. Louis defense stormed in, and Delhomme's option pitch was deflected by Leonard Little.

Delhomme would say later he never should have made the pitch—he just should have accepted the sack and taken a field goal.

"A pretty dumb play on my part," Delhomme said.

After Delhomme made the pitch, Foster made one of the game's most overlooked plays—getting a hand on the bouncing ball just before a St. Louis player running at full throttle picked it up and went 95 yards the other way. The ball bounced mindlessly into the end zone under a swarm of jerseys.

And who came out with it?

Muhsin Muhammad.

Muhammad had an excellent postseason—even making the cover of *Sports Illustrated*—but no play he made was bigger than this one, where he didn't even catch a pass. One of the strongest wide receivers in the NFL, Muhammad wrestled the ball away from several Rams in the end-zone scrum and came out with the ball and holding both hands aloft.

St. Louis challenged the call, but the touchdown was upheld. Carolina led, 7-6.

Cracked Jim Szoke in the Panthers' radio booth: "That's just the way you draw it up."

Donnalley's Flags

One of the strangest sequences of the game took place in the second quarter, when normally reliable offensive guard Kevin Donnalley was called for three major penalties on the same drive.

"Three penalties in four plays," Donnalley says now, shaking his head in disbelief. "I thought about that the rest of the game. If we had lost by a few points, I would have been haunted by that for the rest of my life."

The first flag was for holding, the second for a face-mask penalty and the third for holding again. The Panthers somewhat miraculously overcame those 35 yards in penalties to get a John Kasay field goal out of the drive.

Of the flags, Donnalley says: "One of them was legit. One of them could have been called either way. And the last one— the one where I threw the guy down just by using his own momentum—that was just a plain bad call."

A "Field-Goal Fest"

St. Louis Rams wide receiver Torry Holt was miked up for the game by NFL Films with the idea that he would likely be a critical part of the game and have many things to say about it.

The second part of that was true. The first part wasn't.

Although Holt had been one of the NFL's best receivers during the season, he had almost nothing to do with the game. He had only two catches for 21 yards, dropped a difficult one-handed catch that could have been a 50-yard gain had he dove for it and was also negatively involved in one of the game's biggest plays in overtime.

Holt did have a few funny things to say, though, that were caught on-camera.

"It's a field-goal world! It's a field-goal fest!" he proclaimed as the game wore on into the fourth quarter.

At that point, Holt was right. After Muhammad's touchdown, the game's next five scoring plays were all field goals. Carolina's John Kasay and St. Louis's Jeff Wilkins each had major roles in the game. The Panthers entered the fourth quarter with a 16-12 lead and some good momentum, and the 66,165 fans at the St. Louis Dome started to express frustration that the home team hadn't scored a touchdown yet.

The First 'X Clown'

Early in the fourth quarter, with Carolina still ahead 16-12, St. Louis quarterback Marc Bulger heaved a deep ball over his receiver's head and into the arms of Carolina safety Mike Minter. Minter was tackled at the Panthers' 27, and Bulger left the field to boos. Carolina soon tried out what would be the play of the game for the first time.

The play was called 'X Clown,' and wide receiver Steve Smith would say later he had messed it up at least 10 times in practice that week. On the play, Smith is isolated to one side and has to have time to make a couple of moves.

First, Smith gets off the line and acts as if he's going to cut inside. Then he throws in a hard fake to the outside as if he's going to go deep toward the corner. Then he cuts back to the inside.

With a first and 10 at the Carolina 38, offensive coordinator Dan Henning sent the play in. Smith was alone on the right side. The play was timed beautifully, Smith's fakes were sweet and it worked for 36 yards.

"We knew then we might have a little something," Panthers quarterback Jake Delhomme said later. "Steve ran the route so well."

X-Clown was the key play in Carolina's second touchdown drive of the game, which was capped by a seven-yard burst up the middle by Panthers fullback Brad Hoover (who had carried the ball only six times all season, never for more than five yards).

Carolina led, 23-12, with 8:57 left in regulation.

Martz Gets Cold Feet

The Rams weren't done, though. Even after Marc Bulger threw another interception, they weren't. Carolina got the ball on the St. Louis 28 but failed to score after Tyoka Jackson—who would later play an entertaining part in the overtime coin toss—sacked Delhomme for an 11-yard loss and Kasay missed a long field goal.

The Rams then started to roll. With Marshall Faulk and Isaac Bruce the main weapons, the Rams got down to the Carolina 1 and scored on Faulk's quick cut past Mike Minter on a one-yard run. That made it 23-18 with 2:44 left, and the two-point conversion was good.

Down 23-20, St. Louis needed to recover the onside kick. If the Rams didn't, the game was basically over. In the NFL in 2003, only 21 percent of onside kicks were recovered by the kicking team.

But St. Louis placekicker Jeff Wilkins, who was having a gorgeous game, hit an onside kick so pretty it should have been framed. The ball bounced so high and with such backspin that Wilkins was able to run over and actually recover his own onside kick, giving the Rams the ball on their own 42.

"Holy cow," Wilkins said to himself when the ball started bouncing back toward him.

"You are kidding me," Panthers coach John Fox said in disgust on the sideline.

Immediately, Bulger fired to Bruce for 20 and 13 yards, and the Rams were in field-goal range. A touchdown for St. Louis would now just about seal the game for the Rams.

But once the Rams got to the Carolina 19 with one minute left and a timeout, they inexplicably mashed on the brakes.

The Rams would run only one play in the final minute, and that was a conservative pitchout to Faulk that gained four yards. St. Louis coach Mike Martz never allowed Bulger to take a shot into the end zone.

"It surprised me," Panthers defensive lineman Mike Rucker said. "That's not at all typical of their offense."

Said Fox TV analyst Daryl Johnston over the air: "I never thought I would see Mike Martz play for a field goal and go to overtime."

But that's exactly what he did. Wilkins came on for a 33-yard field goal as regulation ended, and the game went into overtime tied at 23.

Martz would later defend this decision.

"I thought if we got this thing into overtime we could win the game," Martz said. "That's why I did that. I was very sure about the decision and don't regret that decision."

Bulger had thrown two interceptions in the fourth quarter, after all, and Martz was obviously worried about that. Fox also would take Martz's side in the debate, saying later he would have done the same thing in the same situation.

But Fox didn't have Faulk, Torry Holt and Bruce on his side. Martz's decision not to take a couple of shots at the end zone was undoubtedly one of the best breaks the Panthers got all season. It also didn't hurt that Martz never went to his bench for former NFL MVP Kurt Warner, despite Bulger's late-game struggles.

"I Don't Even Know Your Name"

The overtime coin toss was critical. In the NFL's sudden-death format, the first team to get the ball usually wins.

Each team sent several players out to midfield, and St. Louis defensive end Tyoka Jackson immediately started talking smack.

Jackson and Carolina's champion trash talker, Mike Rucker, had already had words earlier in the game. They had passed each other on the field after a special teams play.

"We had a run in," Rucker said. "They were going off the field, we were going on and I started jawing at him. He started yelling, 'We're going to come back. We got you! We got you!' He was the kind of guy that if they had won he would have talked about it forever in the newspapers."

But the Rams had come back. Now Jackson was exultant—and disappointed that Rucker wasn't out there for the coin toss. He turned his mouth on Buckner instead.

"You tell Rucker it's not over," Jackson said. "He thought it was, but it's not. You give him that message."

Buckner looked at Jackson venomously.

"Man, who are you?" Buckner said. "I don't even know your name."

"Your quarterback does!" Jackson replied.

"All right! All right!" the official said, trying to quiet everyone down.

Buckner got to call the toss since the visiting team always has that right. He called "heads" and it was "heads." Buckner may have helped his own cause by giving the coin a lucky blow while it was in mid-air that made an audible "Whoosh."

"We'll take the ball," Buckner said, glaring once more at Jackson before the players returned to their sidelines.

The Delay of Game

The overtime win could have been much less dramatic had the Panthers not mishandled a key situation on their first drive. Jake Delhomme, who led the offense to a wonderful nine-of-17 conversion rate on third downs, converted a third and 10 and a third and eight to get Carolina going. Then Delhomme hit tight end Jermaine Wiggins for 21 yards to the St. Louis 21. Suddenly, Carolina was in field-goal range.

Delhomme took the next snap and moved backward a yard to place the ball in the center of the field. Then Carolina, on second down, sent in the field-goal team.

But a couple of major problems arose. The Panthers believed that the officials didn't get the ball placed quickly enough and that the play clock was started too early. There was no doubt that there were thousands of people in the stadium, including some on Carolina's own sideline, noticing the play clock drifting down to "4...3...2...1" well before the ball was ever snapped to John Kasay.

Delhomme was one of them, but he was 30 yards away on the sideline, unable to scream for a timeout until it was too late. None of the Panthers' coaches nor their players on the field noticed the gravity of the clock situation.

The ball was snapped a couple of seconds after the clock had clearly gone to "zero." Kasay's 40-yard kick split the uprights, but the whistle had already blown. A flag had been thrown, but in the tumult, many hadn't noticed.

Fox ran onto the field, both hands held high.

In the Panthers' radio booth, Bill Rosinski was exultant. His call went like this: "There it is. The placement. Kasay's kick is up, it's on the way... and the PANTHERS ARE GOING TO THE NFC CHAMPIONSHIP!!!"

Then came the mournful voice of Jim Szoke: "No, no, No."

Everyone saw the flag by then. Carolina had to move back five yards.

"They were fooling around with the ball, as far as the spot and getting the game ball back in," Fox would say later, referring to the officials. "I was shocked when they had called delay of game."

Fox decided to run the ball twice more to try to gain back the lost yardage, but that failed.

Kasay came out again, on fourth down, to try a 45-yarder. It hooked right by three inches. Mike Martz, on the St. Louis sideline, yelled in happiness and pulled two fists back to his shoulders.

The game would go on.

Wilkins's Miss

The Rams' best chance to score came on their own first possession of overtime. A 26-yard pass to Isaac Bruce pushed the Rams to the Carolina 38. Then Mike Martz turned conservative again, running Marshall Faulk twice and calling a short pass that was incomplete.

Jeff Wilkins—five for five on field goals already and also with an onside kick recovery to his credit—came on for a 53-yard field-goal attempt.

On the Panthers' sidelines, players held hands. Some turned their heads, afraid to watch.

Wilkins's kick, unlike John Kasay's, was perfectly straight. And about six inches short.

"I don't know if I have been in a game with this much back and forth," Rams running back Marshall Faulk said later. "Emotionally, you're up. You're down. You're up. You're down."

The game would go on.

More Missed Opportunities

E ach team then misfired once more. Carolina drove to the St.
Louis 35 on a 22-yard pass from Jake Delhomme to
Muhsin Muhammad. But Delhomme was sacked twice in the
next three plays.

"On the last one of those sacks, it was totally my fault,"
Panthers center Jeff Mitchell said. "It was one of my worst plays
of the season—the guy [Brian Young] just beat me off the ball
and tackled Jake before he even got set. He was furious."

Delhomme really did almost lose it. He got up, spiked the
ball in frustration and went screaming to the sideline.

"You've got to calm down," Panthers backup quarterback
Rodney Peete told Delhomme. "You're going to get another
chance."

Said Mitchell: "I remember thinking after we got stopped
that time that if we lose this, I'm going to be suicidal."

Delhomme managed to simmer down on the sideline after
a minute. "I'm OK," he told Peete. "I'm OK. I'm calm now. We
just need another shot."

Getting one was no sure thing. St. Louis moved to the
Carolina 38, with a first and 10. But then rookie cornerback
Ricky Manning made a monstrous play. Guarding Torry Holt,
Manning stuck his left hand in between Holt's two hands and
they wrestled for the ball.

Manning somehow yanked it loose from Holt and came
down with a dramatic interception—Bulger's third of the game.

"At first Holt ran a curl route," Manning said. "Then
Bulger hesitated, so Holt converted it to an out route. I went
underneath him on the curl and stayed there when he changed
it. The whole time I was thinking, 'If he throws the ball now, the
ball is mine.'

"Holt got two hands on it, but I got my left hand in
between his two hands and grabbed it out. It was my best interception of the season."

Said Bulger: "I thought worst case it would be broken up because he [Manning] had to go through Torry to get to it. But he made a great play."

Carolina had the ball back. The Panthers lost four yards in two plays—including another vicious sack of Delhomme that had Chris Weinke warming up on the sideline—before the fifth quarter ended.

The game would go on.

Silence of the Rams

The break between the fifth and sixth quarters did Carolina some good. The offense got to talk about what was going wrong—Jake Delhomme had gotten sacked on three of the last five offensive plays.

The Panthers decided to try "X Clown" again, but with wide receiver Steve Smith lined up on the left side this time. With a third and 14 from their own 31, they were just hoping for a first down.

They would also "max protect" Delhomme this time. Instead of the usual five blockers, Carolina would use seven and only send three receivers out into the pattern.

Said Kevin Donnalley: "In my mind, I was thinking, 'We're going to protect this thing up. Jake won't have any pressure. But can somebody get open? That's the question.'"

St. Louis was playing "Cover 2" in the secondary, which is one of the Panthers' favorite defensive alignments as well. It is supposed to prevent the big play, with both safeties lined up deep to make sure that no play gains more than 25 yards or so at the most.

So, on the first play of the sixth quarter, Smith broke off the ball cleanly.

Quickly, he faked out the Rams cornerback, who started veering toward the sideline when Smith swiveled his hips that way. Smith darted back toward the middle of the field and St. Louis safety Jason Sehorn, who was stumbling backwards already.

"Sehorn was a little bit outside the hash," Smith said. "He was a little bit out of position. I broke it in and cut across his face."

Delhomme, with ample time, threw a gorgeous spiral that hit Smith in stride at the 50.

"I braced myself for the big hit, but it never came," Smith said. "And when I took off, I knew I was gone."

Sehorn never touched Smith once he had the ball, nor did anyone else. Smith's pure speed carried him into the end zone, and he held both of his arms outstretched, with his head cocked backward. The pose would later become so famous that the Panthers used it in some of their own ticket-sale advertisements.

"When I did that," Smith said, "it was to say, 'Wow! Look at us!' Not look at me—look at us. What do you think about us now?"

The silence of the Rams was deafening. The entire stadium was quiet except for a few small bands of Panther celebrators.

"Everyone was just standing there with their mouths open, including most of us," Panthers center Jeff Mitchell said.

"I was sitting there on the bench, cramping up, and I was just thanking God that he ran it in," linebacker Dan Morgan said.

Kevin Donnalley, meanwhile, was doing a Jim Valvano imitation.

"I see Steve break free and I'm like, 'He's gone, that's it!'" Donnalley said. "So I'm running down there but I'm too far down, there's no one to hug. I'm not going to run all the way to the end zone—that's too far. So I come back and I grab hold of Todd Steussie."

On the radio, Bill Rosinski could now say it again with vigor: "And we *are* going to the NFC Championship!"

Said Smith later: "I had 28 messages on my phone last week. Fourteen said, 'Good play, good game [against Dallas].' The other 14 said, 'How did you get caught on the 1?' I was going to make sure I didn't get caught this time."

Said Delhomme later: "I threw the ball, but it was really all Steve. I just thought it would be a first down. He made the play. He made the catch. He made people miss. He made the touchdown. It was amazing."

Chapter 8

Philadelphia Freedom

The Carolina Panthers didn't particularly want to play Philadelphia again for the NFC Championship.

For one thing, the Eagles had already beaten Carolina less than two months before. For another, the Panthers would much rather have played the game at home—and for about 24 hours that seemed very possible.

Carolina played St. Louis on a Saturday of a four-game NFL playoff weekend. Philadelphia and Green Bay met on Sunday. If the Packers won, they would have to come to Carolina for the title game. If Philadelphia won, the Eagles would get to host the title game by virtue of their higher play-off seed.

Green Bay led early, 14-0. The Packers led late, 17-14. But then Eagles quarterback Donovan McNabb and wide receiver Freddie Mitchell combined on a miracle.

Needing to convert on fourth and 26 to keep a last-gasp drive alive, McNabb threw a bullet over the middle to Mitchell for 28 yards.

Hearts in the Carolinas started to sink as Philadelphia kicked the game-tying field goal in regulation and then the game-winner in overtime after Green Bay quarterback Brett

Favre threw a horrible interception. The Panthers would have to go on the road *again* to get to the Super Bowl.

Carolina was again the underdog. This was the Eagles' third straight trip to the NFC Championship game, and Philadelphia was 0-2 the past two years. Surely, most oddsmakers and fans outside the Carolinas thought, this would be the Eagles' year.

Inside the Panthers locker room, however, it was a far different story. The Panthers had gained immense confidence in St. Louis. They knew that they had a chance.

And when the Panthers won this game, they had officially made it to the Super Bowl for the first time in team history.

"It's been seven years in the wilderness!" shouted safety Mike Minter right after the game. "When you come out of the wilderness, it feels so good. And guess what? Now it's time to head to the promised land!"

Here's how the Panthers surprised Philadelphia on their home turf, stealing a 14-3 victory keyed by one of the most dominating defensive performances the Panthers have ever put together.

In the Elevator

Eight hours before kickoff, I happened to see Donovan McNabb in the hotel elevator. I was staying at the same hotel as the Eagles, and we rode up from the lobby. It was just the two of us.

The short ride was plenty of time to get a feel for McNabb's lack of jitters. The quarterback was happy and loose. When I asked how he was passing the time, he talked enthusiastically about all the movies he was catching up on in his hotel room. (Evidently, his mother wasn't there to fix him any Campbell's Chunky Soup).

The elevator made a sound like a bell dinging at each floor, and McNabb started to mimic it each time.

"Bom! Bom! Bom!" he said loudly.

Eleven hours later, McNabb would be hurt and subdued in his postgame press conference. His own bell had tolled.

"Peeing On Cotton"

R ight before the Panthers take the field, several players usually address the team to get them fired up. The final spot is generally reserved for Panthers defensive tackle Brentson Buckner, who is an expert at Gipper speeches laced with a touch of street talk.

After the season, Buckner said his speech before the Philadelphia game was his all-time favorite. This is what he said as his teammates clustered around him.

"Everyone's saying we're not supposed to win," Buckner said, glancing around into his teammates' eyes. "It's their stadium. Their third time in the NFC Championship game. All that. But this game isn't pre-destined! We hit as hard as they do! We practice as hard as they do! I want us to take over Philly. I want us to take this whole city and shut it down. By the time we leave this place, I want it to be so quiet that we can hear a mouse peeing on cotton!"

A Cold Night

T he Panthers had brought their cold-weather gear to Philadelphia, which was fortunate. It snowed earlier in the day before the game, and the kickoff temperature at 6:50 p.m. was 33 degrees, with a wind chill of 22.

Most of the players wore long sleeves, but there were several exceptions among the linemen. Philadelphia quarterback Donovan McNabb also opted for short sleeves. Carolina cornerback Ricky Manning, a California kid unused to the cold weather, put on everything the Panthers had in stock. He wore a white ski mask, gloves and long sleeves. Manning looked like a train bandit.

He was about to perform like one, too.

Everyone Say "Shhhh"

The first man to really echo Brentson Buckner's theme of quieting the city on the field was Panthers wideout Muhsin Muhammad. After the game's first four possessions ended in punts, the Panthers began a crisp drive. On third and two from the Philadelphia 39, Muhammad caught a slant pass from Jake Delhomme from 15 yards.

On first and 10 from the Eagles' 24, Delhomme tried Muhammad again. The Eagles brought a linebacker blitz and clobbered Delhomme just as he let it go, and it didn't look like much of a pass. Muhammad was double-covered by Brian Dawkins and Bobby Taylor, and the ball was a wounded duck fluttering to the end zone.

But Muhammad stopped and came back, and neither Eagle touched him. One fell down, one kept running, and suddenly, Muhammad had a touchdown and Carolina had a 7-0 lead.

"I trust Moose," Delhomme said later. "That's what he does. He fights for a ball and he goes and gets it."

Muhammad quickly took a knee in the end zone and put one finger in front of his lips in a "Shhh!" sign—a pose that would make the cover of *Sports Illustrated* the following week.

Carolina wide receiver Muhsin Muhammad caught a 24-yard touch-down pass against Philadelphia to open the scoring in the NFC Championship game on January 18, 2004, then gestured "Shhh!" to quiet the crowd. A similar version of this photo ended up on the cover of Sports Illustrated. *(Photo by Christopher A. Record/*The Charlotte Observer*)*

"It's going to take a whole lot more than that to beat this team, I'll tell you that much!" Moose said into a sideline camera operated by NFL Films.

In fact, it wouldn't.

A McRib Sandwich

The game's most critical play occurred in the second quarter. Philadelphia still trailed, 7-0, but Donovan McNabb had the Eagles on the move, with a first and 10 at the Carolina 23.

As McNabb dropped back, Mike Rucker got a beautiful jump on the snap and joined the quarterback in the backfield. Running back Duce Staley came over to get a panicky partial block on Rucker, but not before McNabb tripped over the two colliding players and fell backward.

The whistle didn't blow. McNair was down at his own 30 and technically could have gotten up and ran, officials would say later.

The Philadelphia quarterback had fallen awkwardly, though. McNabb was rolling onto his back, his left leg stuck in the air, when Carolina linebacker Greg Favors hit him on that leg.

McNabb grimaced, tried to get up and took a knee. The Eagles fans booed. No flag was thrown.

Favors would later defend the hit, saying it was legal since the ball wasn't dead. That was the officials' viewpoint, too.

McNabb came out for one play—he was later diagnosed with torn cartilage in his ribs—and then rejoined the game to thunderous cheers. He completed a 10-yard pass to set Philadelphia up for a field goal. The field goal cut the lead to 7-3.

But after that, McNabb would say later, "It hurt to breathe." The Eagles' franchise quarterback was no longer close to 100 percent.

Shutting Down the Wideouts

On a Charlotte radio station earlier in the week, Panthers rookie cornerback Ricky Manning had made what seemed like a rookie mistake. He had criticized the Eagles receivers he would defend Sunday, saying they didn't impress him at all.

"They didn't seem that fast to me, and they weren't that physical," Manning would explain later.

Manning figured that he could play "press" coverage the entire game against either James Thrash or Todd Pinkston, the Eagles' two starting receivers. Either one, he felt, he could bump around on the line. If he missed the bump, he could still use his speed to catch up.

Manning's theory was first tested later in the second quarter during the Eagles' two-minute drill. On third and seven from the Philadelphia 44, Donovan McNabb threw for Thrash.

Manning instead cut in front of Thrash and made the interception.

"They are coming at me, they are definitely testing me," Manning thought to himself. "All I can say is bring it."

Bringing It

Donovan McNabb didn't have a whole lot of choices in the NFC Championship game. His best running back, Brian Westbrook, had hurt Carolina badly with his speed in the teams' first matchup (a 25-16 Philadelphia win in Charlotte). But Westbrook was out for the playoffs with a torn tricep muscle.

McNabb himself didn't feel like he should run much after the big hit by Greg Favors to avoid getting knocked out of the game. McNabb had run for 107 yards the week before against Green Bay.

So McNabb needed his wide receivers to do something for him, and he figured he might as well test the rookie cornerback again.

Early in the third quarter, with Carolina still holding its 7-3 lead, McNabb directed the Eagles to the Carolina 18. There, on third and six, Todd Pinkston was supposed to run a slant route.

But Ricky Manning was there, anticipating Pinkston's inside cut. Pinkston decided in mid-course to change up and run a deeper pattern.

One problem: McNabb had already thrown the ball.

And Manning picked off another one.

"That's two!" safety Mike Minter screamed into an NFL Films camera. "They better leave him alone!"

Three's a Charm

While the Panthers offense continued to stagnate, the defense kept holding off the Eagles. On Philadelphia's very next series, Donovan McNabb looked for James Thrash again.

This time, the delivery was perfect and would have result-ed in a first down. But Mike Minter separated Thrash from the ball with a huge hit. Ricky Manning was in the right spot again, catching the ball like a pop fly after Minter's assist.

"Dropped right to me," Manning said.

Thrash would say later that Minter hit him so hard he could barely remember the play. Manning had his third inter-ception of the game—the first time in his life at any level of football that he had three in a single contest.

Manning's pickoffs helped contribute to the worst pass rating in McNabb's career. McNabb finally left the game early in the fourth quarter—Philadelphia head coach Andy Reid pulled his quarterback out of the game, fearing he might get injured

*Cornerback Ricky Manning had a breakout performance against Philadelphia to help push Carolina to the Super Bowl. After trash-talking the Eagles receivers earlier in the week, Manning intercepted Philadelphia quarterback Donovan McNabb three times in the game. (Photo by Jeff Siner/*The Charlotte Observer*)*

again. "Donovan would have continued to play until he passed out," Reid said.

When Reid did yank McNabb, the quarterback's rating was 19.3 after he completed 10 for 22 passes for 100 yards and three interceptions. To be fair to McNabb, he wasn't helped by the fact that his receivers dropped six passes.

Foster's Masterpiece

DeShaun Foster had carried the ball 138 times entering the Philadelphia game without scoring a single rushing touchdown. That wasn't what Foster had had in mind when he entered the NFL in 2002. In fact, on Foster's very first carry as a Panther, he sprinted for a 61-yard touchdown, running over standout Washington cornerback Darrell Green in the process.

But that was in a preseason game. Foster then missed the entire 2002 season with a badly injured left knee.

In 2003, Foster had emerged as an able backup and occasional star in the backfield. But he was about to unfurl his best play of the season.

After Ricky Manning's third interception set Carolina up at the Philadelphia 37, the Panthers quickly drove to the Eagles 1. Then Foster got the ball on a pitchout around right end and started a tackle-breaking run that will be emblazoned in the minds of Panthers fans for years to come.

Foster stepped out of one tackle. Bounced off another. Ran through another. Sidestepped another. Dodged another. He broke five tackles in all as he ran parallel to the goal line, trying to push for the single yard he needed.

Finally, after tackle No. 5, he did it. Foster held the ball out in his right hand over the goal-line pylon, and the Panthers suddenly had a 14-3 lead deep in the third quarter.

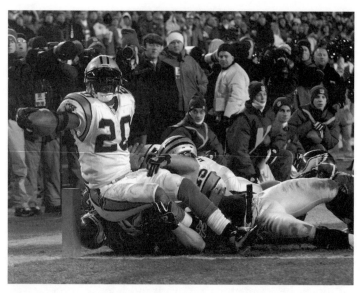

*The longest yard: DeShaun Foster broke five tackles en route to this one-yard touchdown run, his first rushing TD as a pro. Panthers play-by-play man Bill Rosinski said on air that the play took about "a minute and a half." (Photo by Patrick Schneider/*The Charlotte Observer*)*

As Carolina radio man Bill Rosinski described the touchdown: "Oh my goodness! DeShaun Foster on a play that took a minute and a half!"

Running Out the Clock

Carolina would nurse that 14-3 lead the rest of the game. The Panthers would run the ball 40 times and only throw it 14 times in the game. The defense had five sacks, four interceptions and allowed only three points. The offense had scored two big touchdowns.

There would be no final-minute comeback for Philadelphia. The game ended with Jake Delhomme kneeling down three straight times for the Panthers at midfield.

Said offensive guard Kevin Donnalley: "Probably the most emotional I got all season was when we were in the huddle for the Eagles game. There's a minute left, we kneel down and we win it. I'm there with the rest of the offensive guys. So many thoughts are going through my head. For two or three years, it had been so much about the defense here. And how fitting it was that we're the offense, we're on the field, you know, we had outlasted the Eagles and got to run the clock out.

"There were probably nine guys out there who were absolutely giddy. And then [left tackle] Todd Steussie and I, we were kind of emotional. We just looked at each other—we knew how momentous it was. Jake Delhomme didn't know whether to come over and hug me, or try to cheer me up. At that point, part of me knew that the Super Bowl would probably be my last game—that I'd retire, win or lose, after that."

For Delhomme, the best part of the season was also encapsulated in those final seconds and their aftermath.

"If I had to pick just one favorite moment of the whole season, that was it," Delhomme said. "We were out there on the field, knowing we had clinched a spot in the Super Bowl. That time and the whole 30-40 minutes after that, with the team in the locker room. It was like, 'You gotta be kidding me. Is this really happening?'"

Added Mike Rucker: "The next day when you get off the plane you're home and you start thinking about other stuff. But that short period of time at the end of the game in Philadelphia—that was just awesome. I knew all of our families were happy. And I don't mean just the team. I mean the people in Charlotte and the Carolinas. I knew they were having the same feeling we were, and I was proud we were helping them experience that."

Smash Ratings

The Panthers/Eagles game captured the imagination of those in the Charlotte area more than any previous sporting event if you go by the TV numbers. The game drew a phenomenal 50.2 rating and 66 share in the Charlotte area, making it the most watched program in the region's history.

No Headlights

Brentson Buckner took personal satisfaction from the Panthers' bus trip back to the Philadelphia airport after the victory. He had told the Panthers they needed to shut down the city so completely that he wanted to be able to hear a mouse "peeing on cotton" on the drive to the airport, and he claims now that he could have.

"It was so *quiet*," Buckner said. "Driving out of the city, you didn't see a single car headlight. Nothing. That whole place was in mourning. And we were going to the Super Bowl."

Chapter 9

A Stunning Super Bowl

Four days before the Super Bowl, the last remaining original Panther said something prescient.

"I really think it will come down to which team will have the ball last," Carolina placekicker John Kasay said. "That will be the difference in winning and losing the game."

Kasay was right. The Panthers' finest season ever finally ended with a pulsating, 32-29 loss to New England in the Super Bowl on February 1, 2004, in Houston.

Many critics have already labeled that Super Bowl as the best one ever played. It certainly enraptured America—more viewers watched that game than any program in U.S. television history. Nielsen Media Research estimates that 143.6 million Americans saw some part of the game.

It was a very unusual night, punctuated by a very unusual halftime show in which Janet Jackson had her breast bared. There wasn't a single point scored in the first or third quarters. A streaker came out just after halftime, stripped out of his fake referee's costume and cavorted for what seemed like an eternity in front of Kasay as the kicker lined up for the second-half kick-off.

The two defenses dominated for most of the first half—the game was scoreless for nearly 27 minutes, a Super Bowl record. But then the night turned into a rollicking ride featuring Jake Delhomme and New England quarterback Tom Brady trying to one-up one another.

Ultimately, Brady drove the Patriots to a last-second field goal by Adam Vinatieri, breaking a 29-all tie. Carolina would score three touchdowns on its last three offensive possessions, but it wasn't enough.

"Jake Delhomme threw the crap out of it against our defense, which doesn't happen very much," Brady said. "To win it the way we did, it was just incredible."

Said New England coach Bill Belichick: "It was a terrific football game to watch—not a terrific one to coach. I thought I was having a heart attack out there."

If you're a Panthers fan, you understand what Belichick was feeling. The 38th Super Bowl was truly worthy of the word "Super," unlike so many of the previous 37.

Said Panthers coach John Fox immediately after the game: "It's obviously a very big disappointment, but I'm very proud of our football team.... We just came up a little short."

This chapter traces some of the more interesting moments of the Panthers' first Super Bowl, from the pregame hype to the game that actually managed to exceed it.

The Last Time

The lowest on-field moment ever for the Panthers had come only two years before against this same New England team. New England and Carolina played in Charlotte on January 6, 2002, in the final game of the 2001 regular season.

Carolina was 1-14, headed for its worst season ever and less than 24 hours away from firing George Seifert as head coach. New England was rolling, headed toward an eventual Super Bowl win.

New England won in a romp, 38-6. The game was in Charlotte and was witnessed by only 21,070 fans—easily the smallest crowd in stadium history.

It was a surreal scene.

"It was like the sun was shining only on their side of the field," said Carolina defensive tackle Brentson Buckner, who played in the game. "I would never wish what happened to us that day on anyone in the NFL. It was awful."

To John Kasay, the crowd looked even smaller than 21,000. "There were about 15,000 fans, and about 12,000 of them were Patriots fans," he said. "It was a cold, nasty, wet and rainy day. It was just miserable."

A few Panther fans wore sacks on their heads that gloomy, 36-degree afternoon. No wonder. On one of the game's most notable plays, New England rushed only two players and still sacked Carolina quarterback Chris Weinke.

In the fourth quarter, there were maybe 1,000 people in the stands. At least 900 were for the Patriots.

"By the end," Mike Rucker said, "it felt like the whole place was empty except for the Patriots' people."

The game was talked about a good deal by the many players on the Panthers' roster who had participated—20 players were holdovers from the 1-15 team of 2001. They swore it wouldn't happen again.

Media Day

On Tuesday before the Super Bowl, the Panthers faced the national media in force for the first time. Swarmed by more than 1,000 reporters at Reliant Stadium, they were more than happy when they found a familiar face—even if it was Tampa Bay's Warren Sapp.

Sapp, working for the NFL Network, drew a crowd of his own as he drifted into different news conferences to ask ques-

*Five days before the team's first ever Super Bowl game against New England, the Panthers lined up at Reliant Stadium in Houston for a team picture taken by team photographer Kent Smith. (Photo by Patrick Schneider/*The Charlotte Observer)

tions. Muhsin Muhammad told Sapp that one of his greatest pleasures of the season had been beating Tampa Bay twice.

Sapp didn't seem to take offense at the fact that Brentson Buckner had told the world before the season began that Panthers defensive tackle Kris Jenkins had already eclipsed Sapp as a player (and, in fact, that had happened).

Neither Sapp nor Jenkins were particularly good at predicting the future that week, though.

Sapp picked the Panthers to win.

Jenkins didn't say who would win, but did say this: "I really don't see it as such a high-scoring game."

Spelling Test

Panthers quarterback Jake Delhomme was told during Super Bowl week that New England linebacker Tedy Bruschi didn't know how to spell Delhomme's last name.

"That's OK," Delhomme grinned. "I don't know how to spell his, either."

Return of the Linebackers

One of the most emotional moments of Super Bowl week was a press conference in Houston held by linebackers coach Sam Mills and linebacker Mark Fields on Thursday, three days before the big game.

Mills looked thin but determined. He sweated so heavily that one of the Panthers' PR men fetched him a towel.

Fields vowed to return to the playing field again in the summer of 2004 after beating Hodgkin's disease.

Their story was familiar to most Panthers fans. After all, the team had been wearing T-shirts with the players' numbers—51 for Mills, 58 for Fields—under their jerseys on game days all season.

But many in the national media had never heard the story and had never seen Mills nor Fields speak.

Said Fields of the Panthers: "They have been tremendous. They were there with us in our hospital rooms."

Said Coach Fox: "To have the biggest fight of their lives going on and to watch the way they have handled it has been an inspiration to all of us."

Mills had gotten chemotherapy during the Super Bowl week. They unplugged him about 2 p.m. Wednesday and he flew to Houston, where he met with his linebackers about the game plan.

"When they are pumping this stuff into your body, it can be very tough on you," Mills said that day. "You have your good days and your bad days. I am just glad I am having days, you know?"

Smith's Rant

As usual, Steve Smith was working himself into a frenzy before the game. After about the third straight day of questions as to how the physicality of New England's cornerbacks would pose a problem, Smith exploded and delivered a sarcasm-laced rant.

"We're way past the underdogs," Smith said. "We don't even have a shot. I think we just need to pack up now! They've already won, the way you all tell it. We don't even need to be here—this little ol' Charlotte team."

Smith also referred to the upcoming musical performances by Janet Jackson and Beyonce Knowles on Super Bowl Sunday when he said: "It's going to be a big game, and we're going to lose by 14! Go ahead and give them [New England] the rings in the pregame... Everyone can go get their popcorn, watch Janet and Beyonce shake it, and go home."

Asked about some predictions that the game will be a defensive-oriented, boring game, Smith said mockingly: "They're probably right. Carolina football is boring, because we have no playmakers on our team."

Smith also said more seriously that New England cornerbacks Ty Law and Tyrone Poole would have a tough matchup with Smith and fellow wide receiver Muhsin Muhammad.

"There are times when me and Moose have just blocked the cornerback out of bounds, driven the cornerback into the ground—me and Moose have got a few pancakes [pancake blocks] ourselves. Why can't we get any props?"

So what would Smith do against physical corners like Law and Poole?

"I'll do the same thing I did during the season—88 catches, 1,100 yards, seven touchdowns," Smith said.

Smith's First Super Bowl

For many of the Panthers, this was the first Super Bowl they had ever seen. Not for Steve Smith, though.

"As a kid, my Mom was always looking to keep me out of trouble," Smith would say later. "So she put me in the Urban League. Do homework, improve reading skills, stay out of trouble—that sort of thing. They picked 12 kids who were doing pretty good and gave us tickets to the Super Bowl when it was in Pasadena, California [in 1993, when Dallas beat Buffalo, 52-17]. Good seats, too, third row in the end zone. I got to be in the halftime show, too. We were just part of the crowd there cheering Michael Jackson. LA Gear sponsored some of it, and I got a free pair of LA Gear light-up shoes out of it.

"One of the things I got to do that week, too, was to interact with Terry Bradshaw. He was throwing me and some other kids a few passes at this park in Los Angeles a couple of days before the game. He threw me a few bombs and one time he said, 'Man, that kid can *catch*!' That stuck in my head. Years later, I finally got to tell him that. And you know what? He actually remembered me—or at least he acted like he did."

Now That's a Perk

Panthers owner Jerry Richardson wanted to make sure all team employees shared in the Super Bowl week, and he did so with one of the grandest gestures possible.

An e-mail went out to all Panthers employees after the team beat Philadelphia to win the right to go to the Super Bowl. It started: "Congratulations!" It then detailed how each employee would be given two free airplane tickets, four nights in an upscale hotel and two free Super Bowl tickets, courtesy of the Panthers.

From groundskeepers to security guards to secretaries, just about everyone took the Panthers up on it—hundreds of people all told.

The only other team to ever take all of its employees to the Super Bowl, according to the NFL, was Green Bay in 1996.

State of the Union

Jake Delhomme maintained a much lower profile during the two weeks between the championship games and the Super Bowl than did Tom Brady. Brady showed up on magazine covers, all over TV and even in a private box at President Bush's "State of the Union" address, applauding enthusiastically.

With one Super Bowl win already under his belt, Brady seemed confident before the game.

"This is why guys play football," Brady said. "This is the week. This is the game. It defines your playing career—your legacy."

Peppers's Rare Double

The only athlete to ever play in both a Final Four and a Super Bowl is Panthers defensive end Julius Peppers. Basketball, in fact, was Peppers's first love.

Peppers said he noticed more cameras at the Super Bowl. As a lifelong North Carolinian, he still believes that Tar Heel basketball is bigger in the state than the Panthers are.

"But we're gaining on them every day," Peppers said.

Mangum's Memories

Carolina tight end Kris Mangum was thinking about his own father as the Super Bowl approached. He thinks about "Big John" Mangum every year when the Super Bowl is played.

On Super Bowl Sunday in 1994, Kris Mangum was getting ready to drive back to college at Ole Miss when his mother called him from the next room.

"Something's happened to your father!" she said.

Mangum's dad—6-2, 300-plus pounds and a former NFL defensive tackle himself—had had a minor stroke. He couldn't get up and he started to cry—the first time Kris had ever seen his father shed tears.

Mangum called 911. That night in the hospital, Big John and Kris watched some of the Super Bowl together, as Dallas beat Buffalo, 30-13.

Big John Mangum had a major stroke in the hospital not long after that, and he died two months later. Both his sons played in the NFL. Kris's older brother, John Jr., was a defensive back in Chicago.

None of the Mangums made the Super Bowl until Kris did, however. And he was happy to form a different sort of Super Bowl memory this time.

"My dad will be watching this game somehow," Mangum said five days before kickoff. "I know that for sure."

Morgan's Misery

Linebacker Dan Morgan remembered the previous Super Bowl very well. He sat on his couch with his arm in a sling, watching Tampa Bay cream Oakland to end the NFL's 2002 season.

"I wanted to be in the Super Bowl myself," Morgan said. "But things kept going wrong. I couldn't wait to get into the off season and the rehab. It was a depressing Super Bowl for me."

Morgan, at that point, had missed 13 of a possible 32 NFL games due to injury. This time he was rehabbing a dislocated left shoulder, suffered when he made a tackle on Atlanta's Warrick Dunn.

"What has happened to me," Morgan said, "I wouldn't wish on anybody. But it's the kind of thing that makes you into a man."

For six months, Morgan's shoulder really didn't feel normal. Then he had postconcussion syndrome problems in the 2003 season.

But for the playoffs, Morgan was healthy.

And for the Super Bowl, he was one of the few Panthers on defense who could honestly say they played a superb game. Carolina allowed more yards (481) and first downs (29) to New England than the Panthers had in any of the previous 35 games of the John Fox era. But Morgan was everywhere. The coaches' postgame film study credited Morgan with an astonishing 25 tackles—the most any Panther has ever had in any game.

"He was a machine that day," Panthers linebacker coach Sam Mills said.

The Halftime Strip Show

After the game was scoreless for the first 26 minutes and 55 seconds, setting a Super Bowl record for longest 0-0 tie, the offensive fireworks finally began.

In the last 3:05 of the second quarter, 24 points were scored. New England led 14-10 at halftime and the players filed inside the locker room.

A few players who hadn't dressed for the game due to injuries, though, stayed out and watched the halftime show. And what a show it was—it culminated with Janet Jackson having part of her costume stripped off by singer Justin Timberlake to reveal one of her breasts. Timberlake would later blame the "accident" on what he memorably called a "wardrobe malfunction."

Said Mike Rucker: "I actually think the whole Janet Jackson thing has taken away a little bit from the Super Bowl. This was one of the best Super Bowls ever played, and you hate to have that whole issue hanging over it."

Said Brentson Buckner: "That was the first thing I heard about from the guys who stayed out on the field when I came back out—about Janet letting herself hang out there. That was the whole talk on the sideline."

But not for long.

Unless you were in Reliant Stadium on February 1, 2004, you missed this. CBS never showed the Super Bowl streaker, but he showed a lot more skin than Jackson.

The streaker, whose name is Mark Roberts, had done this sort of thing at more than 30 sporting events worldwide. He bought a game ticket legally, then changed into a referee's costume and somehow made his way onto the field.

Roberts then ran in front of John Kasay just as he was about to kick off in the second half, stripped to a G-string and started gyrating.

Players, coaches and referees looked at each other, unsure of what to do.

*Panthers defensive lineman Mike Rucker (93), safety Mike Minter (30) and defensive tackle Kris Jenkins (77) lead Carolina onto the field through the fog just before the Super Bowl on February 1, 2004. (Photo by Christopher A. Record/*The Charlotte Observer*)*

On the Panthers sideline, coach John Fox told one of the Carolina security men: "It's a good thing he doesn't have an Uzi out there, or we'd all be dead."

Despite the tension-filled evening, Fox actually got a laugh out of the whole thing.

"It was like nobody would go get him," Fox said. "But this big, fat naked guy dancing around? Hey, I wasn't about to go get him, either."

Said Buckner: "The funniest thing to me was they hyped up the security for the game. And he sat out there and danced for what seemed like two minutes before anybody came out there."

Eventually, some security men started chasing Roberts. Roberts started running and got leveled by Patriots linebacker Matt Chatham, who gave Roberts one of the best hits of the night, free of charge.

Flipping the Ball

The thing hardly anyone noticed about Jake Delhomme's 85-yard TD pass to Muhsin Muhammad in the fourth quarter of the Super Bowl was the fact that Delhomme actually flipped the football in his hands while dropping back. If you look closely at the replay, the ball does a full 360-degree spin in Delhomme's hands.

"That's something I used to do all the time growing up," Delhomme explained. "When you're playing in the heat and humidity of Louisiana, the ball gets sweaty or your hand does. Subconsciously, I still do it now sometimes, even if I've got a good grip. For quarterbacks, you want everything to be perfect. If I don't like the first grip, I switch it around."

On the play, Muhammad was actually Delhomme's first and last read.

"But I didn't like what I saw at first," Delhomme said. "I came back to look for Steve Smith underneath, but the linebacker was in the way. And what was great about Moose is that he didn't quit. He just kept going. They lost him back there, but I saw him. I threw it as far as I could, and he just made a great play after that."

Said Muhammad right after the game: "I saw Jake heave it up, and I was just smiling when it came down."

"Back to You, Deion"

After Muhsin Muhammad's 85-yard catch gave Carolina a 22-21 fourth-quarter lead, Steve Smith found his teammate on the sideline. Smith then pretended he had a microphone in his hand and started interviewing Muhammad in a bit that was caught on tape by NFL Films.

"All right, Moose!" Smith said. "How do you feel about New England's corners? How do you feel now about how physical they are?"

Said Muhammad, pointing at his chest: "Well, they've been physical to Marvin Harrison and those little guys, but they don't want any of this!"

"OK, back to you Deion, up top!" Smith said.

The name "Deion Sanders" came naturally to Smith's lips—Sanders had been Smith's idol in high school.

Smith would say later that his faux interview was designed to make fun of the media.

"So many people put emphasis on how physical they were, that they knocked Marvin Harrison into the sidelines [when New England beat Indianapolis in the AFC Championship]," Smith said. "I think Marvin Harrison is a great receiver. But obviously he's not physical. I'm not the most physical guy, either. But I'm not going to let another person just do me any way they feel like and just get up and jog back to the huddle.

The interview was just mocking all the media who were hyping the Patriots all up."

The Final Seconds

After Adam Vinatieri's field goal broke a 29-all tie and gave New England a 32-29 lead with only four seconds left, the Panthers were all but done.

Vinatieri's field goal meant that the Panthers literally had some of their prayers dashed.

Said Mike Minter of the moments right before Vinatieri's 41-yarder: "I was praying as hard as I ever have. That's all I could do, pray for him to miss it."

New England only had to keep the kickoff from being returned for a touchdown to ensure the victory. On the sideline, though, Jake Delhomme still felt like Carolina would win.

Delhomme grabbed Steve Smith, who would line up deep alongside Rod Smart for the kickoff.

"If anyone on this field can take the ball back all the way, you can do it," Delhomme said. "Get the ball in your hands. I'll wait for the miracle. Because I really think it's going to happen." Sadly for the Panthers, Smith never even touched the ball. Smart made the questionable decision on the deep kickoff to simply try to score on his own. Smart never got off a single lateral on the play.

The Panthers were also surprised that New England kicked the ball deep. On the sidelines, they were expecting a squib kick.

What If?

The Super Bowl laid every emotion bare, especially in the fourth quarter when a Super Bowl-record 37 points were scored. Carolina was briefly ahead, 22-21, then quickly behind again, then tied the game at 29-all before losing on the last-second field goal.

It turned out to be Kevin Donnalley's final game ever. He would retire a few days later.

"Even during the game when we got ahead," Donnalley said, "I remember thinking that this is so far from being over. I literally just jogged back when we scored, didn't even celebrate. And at the end, I was disappointed. But I also thought, 'What a great game.' Guys played really hard. And it didn't end on something really fluky. Tom Brady did what he was supposed to do, and Vinatieri, a great kicker, put it through.

"They came up a little better that day. But it was a huge disappointment. I know that the rest of my life, during times when I'm watching the Super Bowl or the Panthers, I'll think about, 'What if?'"

Taking Little Solace

Although the Panthers came within a heartbeat of winning the Super Bowl, the players took little solace from that. Coach John Fox had told them repeatedly during the season that the NFL is "only fun when you win." Whether by three points or by 30, they had still lost.

Jake Delhomme was asked shortly after the game if that had been the biggest game of his life. The question was meant as a compliment, since Delhomme had thrown for 323 yards and three touchdowns.

The quarterback didn't take it that way.

"I hope not," he said somewhat angrily. "I don't want to lose on the game of my life."

Steve Smith, who had scored a touchdown for Carolina, also took the loss extremely hard.

"There is nothing accomplished when you don't win," he said. "There's no next week. It's all or nothing, and right now we have nothing."

The Toughest Foes

When I asked Jake Delhomme after the season for this book who he thought were the toughest players he faced all season, he thought carefully about the question.

"Champ Bailey was pretty darn good," Delhomme said of the cornerback, who while with Washington shut Steve Smith down for three quarters of the game. Bailey got traded to Denver in the off season (Smith also believes Bailey is the best cornerback he's ever faced in the NFL).

"Roy Williams, the Dallas safety, was a solid football player," Delhomme continued. "But as a team it would have to be New England—especially that front seven. Those were some big, humongous men."

An (Un)Lucky Number

In Carolina's four playoff games following the 2003 regular season, the Panthers scored exactly 29 points on three occasions. They also did it against Dallas in their 29-10 victory and against St. Louis in the 29-23 double-overtime win.

In football, 29 is a weird number of points. It's also usually a successful one for an offense. "If I had known we were going to score 29 again, I would have liked our chances," Jake Delhomme said. "But it wasn't enough."

In the game, Carolina and New England actually scored four touchdowns and one field goal apiece. But the Panthers missed on two two-point conversions and New England made its one try on a two-pointer, accounting for the three-point difference.

Said coach John Fox: "I don't have any regrets about what we did. We just came up a little short. I've been in two Super Bowls and lost them both. The first time it wasn't close. This time it was. The first time I was ashamed. This time I was frustrated. But it was still a loss. Only one team can go home happy from the Super Bowl.

"Maybe next time," Fox said, "that will be us."

Chapter 10

1995—A First Time for Everything

One of the most entertaining seasons in Panthers history was the very first one, in 1995. It had the feeling of everyone making it up as it was going along, yet the '95 Carolina squad turned out to be extremely good for an expansion squad. It wasn't a Super Bowl team like the Panthers fielded in 2003, but it wasn't bad.

The Panthers played all of their home games at Clemson's Memorial Stadium, 140 miles away, because their own new stadium in Charlotte wouldn't be ready until 1996.

So the Panthers seemed to be always on the road, either by bus or by air. They were led by coach Dom Capers, an obscure defensive coordinator with the Pittsburgh Steelers before Carolina plucked him away. The Panthers cobbled together a mix of veterans and unsure rookies and finished 7-9, even making some noise in the playoff chase in December before fading late.

It was a memorable year in several respects—mostly because it happened at all. Having an NFL team in Charlotte seemed almost unfathomable as recently as the mid-1980s. The city at that time had no professional sports teams and was main-

*In April 1995, quarterback Kerry Collins was introduced as the Panthers' first ever draft pick. Collins started for most of Carolina's first season. The quarterback is shown with Panthers owner Jerry Richardson (left) and then-general manager Bill Polian. (Photo by Christopher A. Record/*The Charlotte Observer*)*

ly known for banking, NASCAR, the downfall of televangelists Jim and Tammy Faye Bakker and the spectacle of pro wrestling.

But eventual team owner Jerry Richardson, a former NFL wide receiver himself for the Baltimore Colts, had built an empire in the food business. He was used to dreaming big. Richardson and Charlotte sports marketing guru Max Muhleman drew up a financial plan that had a key component called PSLs—permanent seat licenses. PSLs were a one-time fee, ranging from $600 to $5,400 per seat, that fans had to pay for the right to buy season tickets.

The NFL (and Panther fans) bought it. At one point, the Carolinas had been listed as a 50-1 underdog in the expansion race in Las Vegas. But on October 26, 1993, the NFL awarded its 29th franchise to Richardson and Carolina.

The team would begin play a little less than two years later, in 1995. Carolina started poorly, losing its first five games. But the Panthers then beat the New York Jets in Clemson behind Sam Mills's interception return for a touchdown of a Bubby Brister shovel pass.

That play, one of the most famous in Panthers history, is discussed in detail in Chapter 13. The shovel pass interception helped propel the Panthers to within an eyelash of .500 in their first season—only a final-day loss to Washington kept that from happening.

This chapter remembers some of the many characters from that 1995 squad, which bonded together so fluidly that the playoffs would become a reality only one year later.

The Promise

The most famous promise in Panthers history came only a couple of days after Jerry Richardson was awarded his franchise. In late October 1993, Richardson spoke to a pep rally in Charlotte that was estimated to include 50,000 fans.

Very few reporters actually covered the event—the main news had already happened, after all, with the franchise being awarded—so many missed the speech. Charles Chandler of *The Charlotte Observer* was there, however, and recorded the words that have been repeated for years back to Richardson.

Said Richardson at the rally: "This is my next pledge to you. Listen very carefully: We didn't get into this for funsies. Our goal is to put together an organization and a coaching staff so that one day we're going to be standing here in this same area celebrating our first Super Bowl."

The crowd started cheering wildly then. Richardson could have stopped. Instead, he waited a few seconds and said: "Wait a minute! You missed the best part. Our first Super Bowl victory, within 10 years!"

Richardson, incidentally, sometimes acts like he wishes he had never said that. When reminded of his pledge by reporters, he often winces.

Road Trips, Part 1

Because even the Panthers' "home" games weren't really at home in 1995, the team sold out only one of eight games that season at Clemson. It turned out that a 280-mile round trip on a Sunday was more than some fans were willing to stomach. Many were also turned off early because of a massive traffic problem on Interstate 85 for the Panthers' first home exhibition game in 1995.

But thousands of fans did make the trip. Tom Broach runs an excellent company called "Broach Sports Tours," which has carried sports fans in the Carolinas to various destinations by bus or plane for years and continues to do so. Broach Sports Tours managed to take 643 people to the Panthers' 2003 Super Bowl, getting tickets for all of them, and that's a major feat because Super Bowl tickets are nearly impossible to come by.

Broach partnered with Muhleman Marketing to operate the Carolina Caravan that season, which was the Panthers' official motorcoach service in 1995. Most NFL teams don't need an official motorcoach service, of course, but that was part of this strange season.

Broach and his employees filled an average of 26 buses per game down to Clemson—about 1,200 fans per contest. Broach was so tickled with this arrangement that after the season he told Panthers president Mark Richardson, the son of Jerry Richardson: "Mark, it'd be a good idea to play a couple more seasons in Clemson."

Said Richardson: "Tom, you're the only person in Charlotte who feels that way."

Road Trips, Part II

The players rode together down to Clemson in buses as well. On the way down, the rookies had to pony up for the food. There was a "fried chicken" bus and a "pizza" bus. As a veteran, you chose your bus based on what food you wanted to eat.

"Carlton Bailey had a lot to do with getting the food on there every week," special-teamer Dwight Stone said. "Carlton was a smooth negotiator."

Most of the time, on the way home from Clemson, the players and coaches were allowed to either take their families on the bus with them or else drive home in their own cars.

"We learned quickly the best way to do that was get your wife or girlfriend on the bus," wide receiver Willie Green said. "The bus was a lot quicker—it usually had a police escort. Without that, you could probably fly to California and back faster than you could get to Clemson and back from Charlotte."

The bus trips are looked upon nostalgically now by most of the Panthers who participated.

Said linebacker Sam Mills: "We had food, old movies playing, friendships forming—it was just so much fun."

Said defensive end Gerald Williams: "Believe it or not, it really wasn't a pain. For the entire team, that was a great time to bond. We really didn't know each other well, but on those bus trips, we got to know each other. And I firmly believe that our 1996 season was so special in large part because we bonded so well in 1995 on the bus."

The Famous First Cut

The Panthers didn't think much of it when they made their very first cut of the roster. So many players were trying to make the team that the squad's temporary practice facility at

Winthrop University in Rock Hill, S.C., needed a revolving door.

The first guy fired was an obscure defensive lineman named Bill Goldberg, out of the University of Georgia. Carolina had picked him in the expansion draft—the 66th choice overall of that draft—but didn't think much of him.

Said Gerald Williams: "I sat in some meetings with Bill. We'd tease each other a little about the Southeastern Conference, since I'm from Auburn and he went to Georgia. For the most part he was a quiet guy, trying to feel his way like most of the younger players. He was a talker, though, whenever he did something good on the field."

That was rare. Goldberg was so unimpressive that he was around for less than two months before getting cut.

Getting fired was a good career move for Goldberg, however. He dropped his first name entirely and became a tattooed, bald, goateed, talkative, rich and very famous professional wrestler.

The First Game

The Panthers nearly won their first ever real game. In a road game against Atlanta, they scored on their very first possession. Quarterback Frank Reich threw an eight-yard pass to tight end Pete Metzelaars for the inaugural Panthers touchdown.

Carolina fell behind 20-13 late, then got a 44-yard pass from Reich to Willie Green to make it 20-19 in the closing seconds.

Coach Dom Capers wanted to go for two points and the win in regulation, but offensive lineman Derrick Graham jumped too soon. After the five-yard penalty, the Panthers were forced to kick the extra point and ended up losing in overtime, 23-20.

The winning quarterback for Atlanta that day?

That's the answer to another trivia question. It was Jeff George.

The Hills Are Alive

One of the Panthers' temporary stars of the 1995 season was running back Derrick Moore. He led the team that year with 740 rushing yards, including the team's first ever 100-yard rushing game.

Moore had a gap-toothed smile, a great enthusiasm for life and a near-obsession with the 1965 Julie Andrews movie *The Sound of Music*. He could quote the lyrics and sometimes would without provocation. He would actually sing *My Favorite Things* to himself when he wasn't feeling good about life. He kept a tape of the movie always at the ready in the VCR.

"Julie Andrews doesn't know how much of an impact she's had on me!" Moore said. "Those other nuns in *The Sound of Music*, they think Julie is being ornery. But she's just following her dreams. Like me!"

Once Moore's love for the movie was revealed in a 1995 story I wrote for *The Charlotte Observer*, Panthers long-snapper and computer whiz Mark Rodenhauser quickly went to work. He took Moore's face and body and superimposed it onto an old *Sound of Music* movie poster, making it seem like it was Moore inside Julie Andrews's dress, twirling happily in the Austrian countryside.

Then Rodenhauser ran off a dozen copies or so of the movie poster and stuck them all over the Panthers' locker room.

Moore was a good sport about it.

"I never knew I'd look so good in a dress," Moore said.

I liked Moore. For that matter, I like *The Sound of Music*, too.

I also thought Julie Andrews might not have many football players who admitted to being huge fans of hers. I found out where Andrews was at the time—in Broadway, starring in a musical—and wrote to her in care of the theater. I enclosed a clipping of the story and a note about how sincere Moore really was.

Andrews provided a happy ending to this story. She sent back an autographed picture of herself to Moore. I gave it to Moore one day after practice, and he beamed with happiness.

Rodenhauser's Posters

Mark Rodenhauser's poster of Moore was hardly his first dabbling in the art of making his teammates look silly via computer. Long snappers have all kinds of time on their hands, and Rodenhauser combined that with a quick wit and the best computer skills any Panther has ever had.

"Rody," as they called him, started making posters almost every week because his teammates looked forward to them so much. So did reporters, who started mentioning them in their newspapers.

Offensive guard Matt Elliott, a smart guy who didn't mind throwing around five-syllable words, was made into the cover of a fake Rodenhauser magazine called "IQ." Rodenhauser placed a fake "Intel" symbol on Elliott's head.

Ed Stillwell, an amazingly gruff security man from the Panthers' earliest years, had a bit of a belly. Rodenhauser made up the cover of a fake cereal box called "Ed Stillwell's Cholesterol Crunch." The cereal supposedly contained "1,000 percent" of the recommended daily allowance of fat, sugar and cholesterol.

"It was both an honor and not an honor to be selected for one of my posters," Rodenhauser said. "I never made them vindictive, but you would get teased about it a little bit."

Rodenhauser eventually found himself in the middle of a small, computer-generated controversy. He poked a little fun at Capers with a spoof called "The Fifth Beatle." It showed pictures of John, Paul, George and Ringo along with a picture of Capers.

Capers didn't particularly like being the subject of a Rodenhauser poster, although the humor was very gentle.

"After that, I was told not to post the posters until late in the week, after the media was no longer allowed in the locker room," Rodenhauser said.

The Replacement Child

I can almost guarantee you've never heard of this next guy, but he provided one of the most amazing stories I ever was privileged to write for *The Charlotte Observer.*

His name was Darryl Moore, and he was one of the "Original 10" Panthers. The Panthers signed 10 players in December 1994, almost nine months before the team would ever play a real game. Most of them got to training camp with Carolina and eventually got cut. Moore was one of those.

But while Moore was briefly a Panther, he told me a story about his family that was so sad, bizarre and ultimately heartwarming that I had to go down and see it for myself.

Moore grew up in the small town of Minden, Louisiana, born to a remarkable woman named Ida Mae Moore.

Ida Mae gave birth to 12 children. Darryl was No. 11.

But only five of those 12 children were still alive when Moore joined the Panthers. Seven had died in various tragedies—four of them in a 1961 house fire caused by a gas explosion.

After that fire, Ida Mae said she prayed to God to give her one child back for each one she lost.

That happened. Darryl Moore was proud to call himself a "replacement child."

"I try to tell people sometimes where I come from, about all that has happened to me and to my family," Moore said. "It's hard. Hard for them to understand, hard for me to tell. But it's important for people to know what we've survived."

Farkas! Farkas!

Another of the "Original 10" Panthers was offensive tackle Kevin Farkas. He was the most physically gigantic Panther I've ever seen—6-9, 347 pounds, a Goliath in cleats.

To watch Farkas run, though, was painful. The Appalachian State product was a plodder, unused to moving more than about five yards per play.

But one of Dom Capers's rules in the Panthers' first training camp in 1995 was that every Panther had to run 14 straight 40-yard dashes in a prescribed time. For the offensive line, the time was 6.5 seconds.

Farkas was having serious trouble.

"I think people heard him dying two states away," Rodenhauser said.

As other players finished their 40s, they all started watching Farkas. Kicker John Kasay started fanning Farkas's face between 40s with a towel.

Others started shouting, urging him on.

"Go, Farkenstein!" sprang up the cheer.

Farkas barely made it back to the starting line for No. 13 of 14. But on the 14th, he mustered some reserve and sprinted to the finish. His teammates happily mobbed him. It was one of the best Panthers' training camp moments ever.

The Cell

The most spartan quarters ever endured by a Panthers head coach was Dom Capers's "cell." That's what Capers called the little room deep in the bowels of Ericsson Stadium where he usually spent three nights a week, starting in the 1995 season.

The Cell had a black leather sleeper sofa with a hunter green comforter that Capers always neatly tucked into the bed's corners after getting up every morning. The walls were gray cinder block. There were no windows. There was a TV, but its screen was always turned toward the wall—by the time Capers went to bed, he was too tired to do anything but sleep.

Capers liked to joke that The Cell was good training for a "minimum-security prison."

The Cell saved Capers about three hours a week. He had a 5,000-square foot house on Lake Norman, 30 minutes away from the stadium, but by staying at The Cell he managed to avoid the commute. Capers had always been somewhat obsessive like that. His family liked to tell the story of when he used to cut lawns back in his Buffalo, Ohio, hometown, and how he would sometimes finish the lawn's edges with a fork to get them just right.

Capers had no children, and for much of the time in Charlotte his wife, Karen, remained on the job as a flight attendant for United Airlines. She knew that if she didn't work, she'd be sitting in her house alone for days at a time.

Obsessiveness

Of all the Panthers' coaches, no one has been so oblivious to the outside world as Dom Capers. In this way he was somewhat similar to former Miami Dolphins coach Don Shula, whom I covered for a couple of years as a beat writer for *The Miami Herald* in the early 1990s.

Shula was undeniably gifted at what he did and really did-
n't pay attention to anyone else. One legendary story about
Shula concerns the time that actor Don Johnson visited practice. Johnson was then at the absolute height of his fame as the
star of the police drama *Miami Vice*, which was the hottest thing
going in Miami.

After practice, Shula was introduced to "Don Johnson of
Miami Vice."

Shula told Johnson, "You guys are doing a great job out
there!"

Johnson said he appreciated it and invited Shula to come
watch them "shoot" sometime.

"Oh, no!" Shula said. "I don't think I need to see that!"

As the conversation went on, it became apparent that
Shula thought Johnson was a real cop, protecting the mean
streets of Miami.

Capers was just like Shula (minus the 17-0 season and two
Super Bowl wins, of course). Once, all of Capers's assistants
failed to show up for a scheduled meeting.

"Did everyone quit?" Capers wondered aloud.

In fact, all of the assistants had huddled by a TV to see the
O.J. Simpson verdict.

When told of the verdict, Capers was relieved that his
assistants were still employed—but he didn't care much one way
or the other about the verdict. Once O.J. wasn't in the league
anymore, Capers hadn't given the former running back a
thought.

The Security Guard

Dom Capers wasn't totally without a sense of humor, however. Once, his wife, Karen, was supposed to pick him up
at the stadium but got delayed because her hair appointment
ran late. Capers slipped into the security guard booth at the

front gate of the stadium, the gate where everyone has to pass in or out on weekdays.

As the players and employees left, they saw Capers alone inside the booth, happily waving at each of them.

"What are you doing?" they would ask.

"I'm taking on some extra responsibilities," Capers shouted.

Polian's Power

The early Panthers were formed mostly by team president Mike McCormack and general manager Bill Polian.

While McCormack was a warm, soft-spoken man and already an NFL hall of famer for his playing career as an offensive tackle, Polian was tempestuous, especially when negotiating contracts. He had a dislike/hate relationship with sports agents. He would occasionally use the line, "I'm going to come through this telephone and tear your tonsils out!" to particularly stubborn ones.

When Polian realized in 1996 that a sympathetic movie about a sports agent called *Jerry Maguire* was being made, and that the agent would be played by Tom Cruise, Polian said: "The apocalypse is upon us."

The Virgin Fullback

The Panthers' first team also included Bob Christian, who had one of the most appropriate surnames in sports.

Christian was an advocate of saving sex for marriage. In 1995, he was 26 years old, had never married, was very religious and was still a virgin. Christian said it was very important to him to make a sexual commitment only to his wife, saying society had "cheapened sex" and that was one reason why the divorce rate was so high.

It might surprise you to know that in the locker room Christian wasn't teased much about his beliefs. Occasionally, someone would note one of Christian's standout blocks and say that it looked like Christian was hitting somebody so hard because he needed some sex, but generally the other players didn't argue with him.

Christian was a good player for the Panthers that season. He had more than 400 total yards and did score—his first career touchdown, that is.

Merry Christmas

A s a sportswriter, you understand quickly that working on weekends is part of the job. Holidays sometimes go out the window, too. Early in my newspaper career, I often worked on Thanksgiving Day. The Carolina Panthers always practiced that day, so somebody from the newspaper had to go. I remember bringing Dom Capers a piece of homemade pumpkin pie to one interview—I think he took it back to The Cell to eat it.

The weirdest holiday I've ever spent related to the Panthers came at the very end of the 1995 season. Carolina had just lost, 20-17, to Washington on December 24, 1995, to finish a 7-9 season.

The game ended so late in Washington that I couldn't get home until Christmas morning. But the rent-a-car place wasn't open to return the car I had rented. It was Christmas, after all.

In a quandary about what to do, I explained the situation to the person at the front desk of my hotel.

Very nicely, the guy told me to leave the car in the hotel's underground parking deck, the keys at the front desk and the phone number for the rent-a-car company. When they opened in the afternoon, he would call them and they could come pick the car up.

I wished him "Merry Christmas" and flew home without incident. But that afternoon, I had a strange feeling about it. I called the rent-a-car company to make sure they had gotten the car back as scheduled.

"What car?" the man said.

Uh-oh.

I spent most of the rest of that miserable Christmas Day was spent on the phone. It turns out the guy at the hotel front desk got off work about 30 minutes after I had checked out, and he had decided to take the rent-a-car on a little joyride—from Washington to Philadelphia. He figured no one would miss it.

The car eventually made it back to Washington OK. The guy who took it got fired.

And the Panthers' first season—for its players and for me—was finally over.

Chapter 11

1996—A Glorious Season

The Carolina Panthers only had two winning seasons in their first nine years. The second, of course, was their Super Bowl season.

The first still occupies a sweet spot in the minds of many Panthers fans and players who were involved in it. The 1996 season—only Carolina's second in the NFL—saw the Panthers hum to an overall record of 13-5.

It was an extraordinary season for a second-year team—and one that would cause all sorts of unrealistic expectations for years to come.

The Panthers opened their new stadium in 1996 by going 9-0 at home—8-0 in the regular season and 1-0 in the playoffs. Every game sold out. Most of them boasted Carolina-blue skies with a few puffy clouds and temperatures in the 60s.

Not only did the Panthers win the NFC West by dispatching San Francisco twice, they also secured a first-round playoff bye (something the 2003 team couldn't do). They did that by edging Pittsburgh in the final regular-season game with an end-zone interception by safety Chad Cota.

The 1996 team was built on defense, a ball-control offense and strong unity throughout the team. Second-year quarterback Kerry Collins was kept on a fairly tight leash by the coaching staff but did make critical throws in several wins. Running back Anthony Johnson not only was a 1,000-yard rusher but also played on all of the special teams. Three of the four starting linebackers—Kevin Greene, Sam Mills and Lamar Lathon—earned Pro Bowl recognition.

The 1996 Panthers were a poised team, and that was never more evident than in their 30-24 win at San Francisco deep in the regular season. Said then-49ers coach George Seifert after the game, in which San Francisco had a team-record 15 penalties for 121 yards:

"We came unglued. We got too caught up in the 'in-your-face' football. They appeared to be the team with all the tradition and poise, not us."

Maybe that Carolina win should have given the Panthers a clue that it wasn't such a great idea to hire Seifert as their coach two years later when Dom Capers ultimately got fired. Seifert, in fact, was only 1-3 against the Panthers while coaching the 49ers.

The 1996 Panthers team ultimately peaked with a 26-17 home playoff win against Dallas in January 1997—a victory that pushed Carolina into the NFL final four. The Panthers then had to go to Green Bay for the NFC Championship. There they were frozen out, 30-13, behind a Packer squad led by quarterback Brett Favre. That was a great Green Bay team—one that would ultimately win the Super Bowl over New England—and possibly the only team in the NFL that was better than the Panthers in 1996.

A Near-Wreck With Elway

Quarterback Kerry Collins got into plenty of scrapes during his brief tenure with Carolina. One of them, though, was just good for a laugh. The Panthers went to Colorado in the summer of 1996 to train with the Denver Broncos for a few days during the long preseason, and it was there that Collins became acquainted with Denver quarterback John Elway.

Once, Elway was hurrying Collins and several other Panther players back to a team meeting on a golf cart after they had all eaten at a Mexican restaurant together. Collins was in the back with nothing to hold onto, and Elway was scooting the golf cart around the Northern Colorado campus like he was running a two-minute drill.

Collins told him to slow down.

OK, Elway said. But then Elway hit one more curve at full speed.

Collins toppled out and rolled over and over in the asphalt parking lot.

Panic-stricken, Elway slammed on the brakes and ran over to Collins. Are you OK?

Collins was OK that time, except that he scraped his hands on the asphalt.

Salt and Pepper

Before there was ever Julius Peppers for the Carolina Panthers, there was Salt and Pepper. That was the moniker Lamar Lathon and Kevin Greene attached to their sack partnership, which had its most successful year in 1996.

That season Greene had 14.5 sacks and Lathon had 13.5, crashing in from their outside linebacker spots in Dom Capers's 3-4 defensive scheme.

*Linebacker Kevin Greene exults after knocking down San Francisco quarterback Steve Young. The Panthers defeated San Francisco twice in 1996 on the way to a 13-5 record and the NFC Championship game. (Photo by Christopher A. Record/*The Charlotte Observer*)*

Both were fan favorites. Lathon was famously insecure, tremendously talented and boasted the most perfect football body I've ever seen in a Panthers locker room as long as you overlooked the knee scars. Greene was a great on-field showman who dabbled in pro wrestling as well, with his long blond locks and his knack for the quarterback.

Before many games, teammates said Greene would crack open a can of tuna and eat it. Lathon was famous for arriving fashionably late so people could check out his new threads, which were usually Italian and always expensive.

Capers sometimes joked that Lathon and Greene both bowed to what he called the "sack god." They were each very aware of their stats. In the opening game of the 1996 season, Lathon had three sacks to Greene's two and then fretted because Greene got far more attention after the game (mainly because Greene's sack dances had been a bit more inspired).

Mostly, though, the two got along.

Said long-snapper Mark Rodenhauser: "Those guys were really good athletes, but even though you might think otherwise, they really weren't 'me-me-me' type egos. They were quite content to be part of the team. Even Kevin Greene, who was very gregarious and outgoing, he was team first. And although Lamar Lathon would take all the attention he could get, he didn't actively go after it."

Said special-teamer Dwight Stone: "Kevin was Mr. Football. Outside of Sam Mills, he was the most professional guy on the 1996 team. He made Lamar better by pushing him. Kevin and Lamar were the only two that could get away with calling Mr. Richardson 'Big Cat.' They started that long before some guys on the 2003 team did it."

Lathon's Legacy

amar Lathon did a number of memorable things on the field for the Panthers. For instance, early in the first quarter of the Panthers' playoff game against Dallas following the 1996 season, Lathon fractured Michael Irvin's shoulder with a clean, incredibly hard tackle. That changed the entire dynamic of that game and put Irvin on the sideline in a gold, six-buttoned suit and sunglasses.

Said defensive end Gerald Williams, a Panther from 1995-97: "In 12 years in the NFL and all my other years around football, I've only been around two people with unbelievable athletic ability. The first was Bo Jackson. We were the exact same year at Auburn, and I thought I'd never see anything like Bo again. But then along came Lamar Lathon. I had never seen a 265-pound man run a 4.5 40 until I saw Lamar."

Lathon was just as memorable off the field. Money poured through his fingers—sometimes to family members or total strangers in crisis, sometimes to auto dealers.

Said wide receiver Willie Green: "The most memorable person I remember on that 1996 team was Lamar. He was the best pure athlete on those early teams. He had amazing muscles, and he didn't mind showing them off, either. He'd buy a $200,000 car, and then he'd get the matching luggage to go along with the car."

Remembered Williams: "Lamar had a new car every other month, and they weren't cheap ones, either. He had a Dodge Viper with an embroidered Panthers head on the seat. I think that one had black-and-blue inside trim, too. He had a Mercedes sedan. He had a Ferrari. He had a Range Rover. And somewhere in there, he had a Rolls Royce."

Said Dwight Stone: "L.L. was something else. If you were a young guy in the NFL, he was what you wanted to be like. A single guy, expensive suits, women always around, fast cars—he lived the fantasy life."

The Snarling Statues

The most popular camera spot at Bank of America stadium, which opened in 1996 as "Ericsson Stadium," has always been the Panther statues. There are six of them—two apiece at each of the stadium's three primary entrances.

They weigh 2,800 pounds apiece and are 22 feet long. They are coal black in color, except for their green eyes. Around Christmastime every year, they each get a Christmas wreath collar.

Team owner Jerry Richardson has occasionally used the statues as a metaphor in speeches to the players, saying he wants them to look at the statues occasionally if they are ever in doubt as to what a true Panther should be like on the field.

Billy Graham's Crusade

One of the most heavenly moments at the Panthers' stadium—and certainly one of team owner Jerry Richardson's favorite all-time moments—came without a football in sight.

In September 1996, Rev. Billy Graham appeared for a four-night crusade at the new stadium.

Graham has deep Charlotte roots and also has a major road in Charlotte named for him. The evangelist had officially dedicated the stadium on August 17, 1996.

On the opening night of his crusade that September, Graham proclaimed before more than 65,000 believers: "There's no stadium so beautiful and state of the art as Ericsson Stadium here in Charlotte. God bless you, and God bless the Panthers."

Tough Guys

That 1996 team had some of the toughest players the Panthers have ever employed as well. Ask members of the team to vote on who was the toughest and several different names come up.

Said Willie Green: "It has to be fullback Howard Griffith. This guy probably had about two concussions a game. He had back injuries, neck injuries, arm injuries—but you never knew he was hurt. That was just routine for him."

Said long snapper Mark Rodenhauser: "One of the guys who just didn't quit no matter what was Anthony Johnson. He was very tough."

Said linebacker Sam Mills: "I'd have to go with either [nose tackle] Greg Kragen or [safety] Brett Maxie. I really admired them both. Kragen just gave you everything he had. He wasn't the greatest athlete in the world, but he had such great effort. And Maxie was a very smart, tough player who meant a lot to the defense and didn't get enough credit."

Said defensive end Gerald Williams: "It had to be Sam Mills. He was the absolute backbone of that team, and no one has ever been more mentally tough than he was."

Agreed special-teamer Dwight Stone: "Sam Mills—he was strong all over. Mind, body, heart, communication skill. You loved to go to battle with him, because you knew he wasn't going to leave you behind. The guy didn't have a single weak spot—other than being short."

High School Teammates

One of the coincidences of the 1996 season was the fact that kicker John Kasay and wide receiver Willie Green had played together before—not in college, but in high school.

The two were teammates on the Clarke Central High team in Athens, Georgia. But they weren't particularly close friends there. They would get closer once they joined the Panthers.

"John hung out with the preppy guys—the ones with a penny in their penny loafers, argyle socks and an alligator on their shirts," Green said. "I hung out with the black guys in the cafeteria."

Watch That Hamburger

One of the more purposely irritating Panthers in the locker room over the years was special-teamer Michael Bates. Bates had astonishing speed. He won a bronze medal in the 1992 Olympics in Barcelona in the 200-meter dash. He was also a tough football player who was such a good special-teams player that he set a Panthers record with five straight Pro Bowl selections from 1996-2000. In 1996, Bates averaged an amazing 30.2 yards per kickoff return, the highest in the league since 1977.

For all that, though, Bates acted like he was nine years old.

"Michael was a great athlete and a little kid," laughed Dwight Stone, a fellow special-teamer and one of Bates's best friends. "People would actually come up to me and tell me to stop Michael from playing so much. I had to babysit him. Say you're eating a hamburger and really enjoying it. Bates would walk by and slap it out of your hand and just keep walking. After a shower, you'd go out to find your towel and he would have used it and then hung it back up in the same spot. You know that one little kid in every neighborhood that nobody wants to play with because he just keeps bothering you all the time? That was Bates."

The Good Hands Man

The best target near the end zone that season was Panthers tight end Wesley Walls, who scored 10 touchdowns in 1996. Walls was a Southern-fried storyteller from Mississippi, and he also had the best pure hands of any Panther who has ever played.

"That's true by far," said Dwight Stone, a Panther special-teamer and wide receiver from 1995-98. "Mark Carrier would be No. 2. Wesley made incredible catches. When you saw them in slow motion, you couldn't believe the body control. I also have thanked him many times for getting me hooked on deep-fried turkey at Thanksgiving."

Walls was also one of the most egocentric players on the team. He wanted to make sure he was heavily involved in the gameplan every week and fretted publicly when he wasn't. But when you threw him the ball, he usually delivered. The Panthers finally released him before the 2003 season, but when he was released he was the team's all-time leading touchdown scorer with 44.

Brockermeyer's Tips

Blake Brockermeyer was an offensive tackle from Texas, a place where football is hard-wired into everyone. He was a first-round draft pick of the Panthers in 1995 and reporters quickly found that among Brockermeyer's passions were cigars (he would take the magazine *Cigar Aficionado* on team planes) and proper behavior by football fans.

Brockermeyer quickly found in Carolina that the fans didn't cheer quite when they should.

Brockermeyer tried to lead cheers from the sideline and then wrote a brief story that appeared in *The Charlotte Observer,* coaching fans on how to cheer.

Among Brockermeyer's "commandments":

—Don't leave the game if it starts raining.

—When the Panthers offense is on the field, don't do the wave.

—Boo the officials every time they call a penalty on the Panthers.

The Rocket Man

One of the oddest players ever to grace the Panthers' locker room was Raghib "Rocket" Ismail, the speedster from Notre Dame.

Ismail almost quit the Panthers before he ever got started. When they traded a fifth-round pick to Oakland for him in August 1996, he almost decided not to come. General manager Bill Polian talked him into trying it, and once Ismail came he gave the Panthers a new string of stories to tell.

Ismail was not one of those players who fought through every ache so that he could make every single snap of every practice. Once, he said he was overcome by fumes on the practice field.

At every practice at that time, the Panthers sent two men to videotape practice up into the sky via a large tower powered by a portable generator. On this day, the generator had malfunctioned and spilled gas on the grass. Some practice groups did move away from the gas fumes, but only Ismail was overcome by them. He asked for, and received, permission to sit out the rest of practice because he felt "queasy."

Sir Purr's Punt Return

A graphic once flashed on ESPN that was correct but requires some explanation. It read: "SIR PURR. Punt Returns: One. Yards: Zero."

Sir Purr is the Panthers' mascot. He's a six-foot-tall black cat (the fact that the Panthers' mascot was a black cat also made for many jokes during the down years from 1997-2002).

Sir Purr has been played by several different people over the years, but the first Sir Purr was Tommy Donovan. Donovan had played "Cocky," the South Carolina Gamecock mascot, for three years before taking over the Sir Purr role. Donovan was always enthusiastic—and, once, a little overzealous.

As a Rohn Stark punt bounced in the end zone during the Panthers' final game of the 1996 season, against Pittsburgh, Donovan watched the football. The ball was dead, right? Had to be. Stark—who liked to say the "h" in his first name was for "hangtime"—had put too much gas on this one.

So Sir Purr dove on the ball. One problem. Until a player touches a punt in the end zone, it is alive and still in play.

"Way to down that punt!" several players told him.

The referee approached Sir Purr, who futilely tried to hide behind a goalpost.

The referee reprimanded Sir Purr, but didn't penalize the Panthers 15 yards, which he could have done.

On the other sideline, Pittsburgh coach Bill Cowher was weak from laughing—so much so that he didn't even protest the lack of a flag.

Beating the 'Boys

The Panthers' first ever home playoff game came on January 5, 1997, against Dallas. In 2004, almost seven years to the day of that game, the Panthers would host Dallas in the playoffs again.

Until that moment in 2004, however, the Dallas playoff win stood as the pinnacle of Carolina's success. It was a major success for the Panthers, who had played in zero playoff games compared to Dallas's 51 entering the game.

Most fans who were there remember the conditions as perfect, and they actually were. For a 4 p.m. start, the temperature was 67 degrees with a 15-mph wind.

Carolina would end up winning 26-17, on two Kerry Collins touchdown passes, four field goals by John Kasay and some inspired defense. Running back Anthony Johnson outgained Emmitt Smith in rushing yardage, 104-80.

The best touch came after the game. Wide receivers Mark Carrier and Willie Green had a great idea—to go back out onto the field and thank the fans. The team slowly circled the field, giving high-fives to everyone it could reach.

Seven years later, John Fox thought that was such a good idea that he had his team do the same thing after Carolina won another playoff game against Dallas.

Switzer's Mistake

Before the Dallas-Carolina playoff game, then-Cowboys coach Barry Switzer said in an interview that Dallas had never been that far south for a playoff game.

Since Charlotte is actually northeast of Dallas, this became big news in the Carolinas. Charlotte has suffered from an inferiority complex for years anyway, and the very idea that the opposing coach might not be able to locate the city on a map was somehow disconcerting and sadly familiar to the populace.

Switzer would say months later that he misspoke and had actually been to Charlotte a number of years before. But Lamar Lathon didn't know that when he spoke feverishly to the television cameras following Carolina's win.

"Now I propose a question for you, Barry Switzer!" Lathon screamed. "While you're sitting at home next week, do you know where Charlotte, North Carolina is now, BABY!"

A Presidential Postponement

Panthers fever was so high during the 1996 season that it even reached the White House. President Bill Clinton postponed a January cabinet meeting so that Erskine Bowles—Clinton's chief of staff and also a Charlotte investment banker—could see the Panthers in the playoffs.

Favre's Time

The Panthers' extraordinary run in the 1996 season finally came to an end mostly due to one man—Brett Favre.

Favre had gotten hooked on the painkiller Vicodin during the 1995 season and stayed in rehab 45 days in early 1996 after admitting his addiction. He came back very determined and said at his return press conference: "You know I'm going to beat this thing. I'm going to win a Super Bowl.... And all I can tell people if they don't believe me is: 'Just bet against me.'"

It wasn't wise to bet against Favre that season. In a game that began with an actual temperature of three degrees and a wind chill of minus-17, Favre actually started slowly. He threw an early interception to Sam Mills that led to Carolina's only touchdown and a 7-0 Panthers lead.

But Favre eventually got rolling, throwing for 292 yards and two touchdowns against Carolina. He completed one pass by shoving a two-handed throw from his stomach just before getting sacked. The Panthers lost, 30-13, in the NFC Championship game.

The Crumbling "Dynasty"

When the Panthers arrived back in Charlotte that night after the loss to Green Bay and went to the stadium to get their cars, there were 3,000 fans waiting for them. Some of the players made speeches and signed autographs for the fans.

Quarterback Kerry Collins said the thing that everyone remembered the most. Collins was boyishly enthusiastic at the time. He had just turned 25 years old and his future problems in Carolina were nowhere in sight yet. He had a great arm and an engaging personality. His future, like the Panthers, seemed limitless.

So Collins just said what people were feeling that night.

"What you've witnessed," the quarterback intoned, "is the beginning of a dynasty."

In fact, it was nothing like that.

Little did Collins or anyone else know, but the Panthers were about to embark on a six-year trip of frustration.

Chapter 12

1997-2002—The "Between" Years

After the Carolina Panthers' surge to the NFC championship game in 1996, confidence in the Carolinas soared. Carolina was a trendy choice to go to the Super Bowl in 1997. The team had a stalwart defense, a fine young quarterback in Kerry Collins and unquestionable fan support.

Then the bottom fell out.

From 1997-2002, the Panthers failed to put together even one more winning season. Two head coaches got fired in that six-year span—Dom Capers and George Seifert. And the team set an NFL record in 2002, Seifert's final year, by losing 15 consecutive games in a single season to finish 1-15.

"Some of the bad times seemed like they lasted an eternity," Panthers owner Jerry Richardson said in late 2003.

There were nasty off-the-field headlines as well. Rae Carruth, the Panthers' No. 1 draft choice in 1997, was found guilty of conspiracy to murder his pregnant girlfriend in a shocking trial shown live for weeks on *Court TV*.

Fred Lane, once a star running back for the Panthers, was killed by his own wife in Charlotte in 2000. Lane had been traded to Indianapolis by then, but everyone still associated him with the Panthers.

*The Panthers had six consecutive seasons without a winning record from 1997-2002, in part because of their poor drafts. Neither quarterback Kerry Collins (12) nor running back Tshimanga Biakabutuka (21) ever fulfilled their potential in Carolina—Collins mostly because of off-field issues, Biakabutuka due to injuries. (Photo by Christopher A. Record/*The Charlotte Observer*)*

Collins flamed out in Carolina due to personal problems, mostly caused by alcohol. He eventually straightened out his life and resurrected himself with the New York Giants, leading them to a Super Bowl.

The Panthers also made some horrendous personnel decisions. They essentially gave up two No. 1 draft picks for defensive tackle Sean Gilbert, who was no more than a mediocre player in Charlotte. They gave a huge contract to defensive end Chuck Smith, whose knee was already shot. They messed up one No. 1 draft pick after another—Carruth, defensive end Jason Peter and defensive back Rashard Anderson were three of the worst. Peter did at least provide one of the best "dazed and confused" quotes in Panthers history, saying at one point during his struggles: "I really don't even know how much I know and don't know."

Those six "between" years weren't without happy moments, either. Steve Beuerlein's quarterback draw against Green Bay is still rightly remembered as one of the best plays in the team's history. The Panthers put together a few victories like that over the six-year span, although too frequently they would win one game in spectacular fashion and then lose their next three.

"You had to laugh to keep from crying," cornerback Eric Davis said during this long period.

Exactly. There were tears and chuckles during the stretch, when the Panthers went 34-62 overall and never qualified for the playoffs. This chapter bulges with stories from those seasons—some of them funny, some of them painful.

Beuerlein's Draw

In those six inconsistent seasons, the undeniable on-field highlight came in Green Bay on December 12, 1999. The Panthers and Packers locked themselves into a thrilling regular-

*There were some fine moments in the "between" years. None of them were better than Steve Beuerlein's five-yard quarterback draw for a touchdown to beat Green Bay at Lambeau Field on December 12, 1999. (Photo by Jeff Siner/*The Charlotte Observer*)*

season game, one that would include nine lead changes and more than 750 yards of total offense.

It eventually came down to one play. The Panthers had the ball on Green Bay's five-yard line, trailing 31-27. A field goal would do no good—Carolina would have to go for it.

It was then that the Panthers ran one of the most stunning, successful plays in team history. Quarterback Steve Beuerlein, whose plodding mobility was roughly equivalent to a mastodon's, dropped back.

Then he ran forward.

It was a quarterback draw—a play that certainly Brett Favre might run, but that no one expected Beuerlein to.

As George Seifert would later describe it (and this was the happiest I ever saw Seifert after a Panthers game), Beuerlein juked, high-stepped and then jumped into the end zone. He scored with about six inches to spare, and Carolina won, 33-31.

"We're going to run the option next week," Seifert joked in his postgame press conference.

The cheeseheads streamed out of Lambeau Field that day, stunned about the loss and the way it occurred. I still remember vividly walking behind a couple of them on the way down to the locker rooms to do some interviews, and one cheesehead saying to another mournfully: "What just happened?"

The Blanket

One of the weirdest heroes in Carolina Panthers history was Israel Raybon. In 1997, Raybon saved a game—and then got fired 22 days later.

Raybon, a nondescript 300-pound, third-team defensive lineman, tipped away a ball against St. Louis on fourth down to punctuate a Panthers' goal-line stand that earned Carolina a 16-10 win on November 23, 1997.

In reality, Raybon was out of position on the fourth-and-goal play from the Carolina 1. He had been blocked so well, all the way into the end zone, that he basically stumbled into the route of Mark Rypien's pass.

"If you're out of position, you better make a play," Carolina cornerback Eric Davis said.

And Raybon did, theorizing later that he probably should have picked the ball off instead and rumbled 108 yards.

Raybon also gleefully nicknamed himself "The Blanket" after the game for his coverage abbility. *The Charlotte Observer* headline the next day read: "Panthers Find Ray of Hope."

Raybon started taking himself very seriously, wearing a T-shirt that read, "I'm 'Bout It."

Three weeks later, the Panthers cut him, tossing away "The Blanket."

Kerry's Heart

In 1998, Dom Capers and Kerry Collins both mishandled a tough situation.

By year's end, both were gone.

Collins and Capers had teamed together nicely for most of three seasons prior to this moment. Capers inserted Collins into the starting lineup during the fourth game of Collins's rookie year and had let him make his mistakes while nurturing the incredible arm that made Collins the Panthers' first ever draft pick in 1995. In 1996, Collins's best season, the Panthers got to the NFC Championship game.

In 1997, Collins's personal life started unraveling. His unabashed bar-hopping was noticed by more teammates. He used a racial slur in the presence of several teammates and had to apologize many times for that (although, to a man, Collins's former teammates will tell you they don't think Collins was actually a racist).

Then, in 1998, everything came apart.

Collins's final game with the Panthers was a 28-point loss to Atlanta on October 4, 1998. After that game, Collins came into Capers's office and, according to the coach, said his heart was no longer into quarterbacking the Panthers.

Capers's exact statement was this: "Kerry said his heart wasn't totally into what he was doing."

It wasn't a smart thing to say.

But Collins was an emotional quarterback—always intro-spective and at the time a bit unstable. He needed help. Plus, he was still a valuable commodity—a 25-year-old quarterback who was once the No. 5 overall pick in the draft.

Capers thought he was helping his team by what he did next, but in reality it helped Capers get fired.

Within a week, Capers had first demoted Collins to third team and then waived Collins outright—basically throwing him away. Even when Collins later tried to amend his statement, saying his heart was into football after all, Capers didn't budge.

Said Capers at the time: "I don't think you can take something back when you're in a leadership position and all of a sudden it's out there. It's hard to take it back once it happens."

Collins would remain somewhat attached to Charlotte, even marrying a woman from the area. But he wouldn't find his stride in the NFL again until he stopped drinking and grew up, which he did with the New York Giants.

Said Dwight Stone, a Panther special-teamer from 1995-98: "I think we all shared some fault with Kerry. I enjoyed the guy a lot. He was a great guy and got caught up in some bad things, but I really think some of us older players should have done more with him as far as trying to guide him toward the right path."

Capers got fired at the end of the 1998 season, when the Panthers went 4-12, but he eventually worked his way back into another head-coaching job with the Houston Texans.

Incidentally, both Capers and Collins were engaging, honest men. I liked both of them. They just messed 1998 up. Badly.

The Trade That Never Happened

Six months before the Capers/Collins fiasco of 1998, the Panthers tried to make a trade that could have changed the course of the franchise.

Carolina started dealing with Indianapolis, which held the No. 1 pick in the 1998 draft. The Panthers were willing to ship

Collins to the Colts, where he would have been the starting quarterback, along with several other starters. The Panthers were willing enough to do the deal that almost no one on the roster was off limits to Indianapolis.

But the Colts and Panthers ultimately couldn't work out a trade.

If it had happened, Carolina had its heart set on drafting Peyton Manning.

Instead, that's the quarterback the Colts would get.

The Carruth Conviction

No Panther has ever done anything off the field nearly as bad as what Rae Carruth was convicted of doing. In January 2001, Carruth was sentenced to at least 18 years and 11 months in prison for conspiracy to murder his pregnant girlfriend, Cherica Adams, in 1999. Adams died after being shot. The baby, Chancellor, lived but has cerebral palsy and has had other developmental issues related to his traumatic birth.

I won't go into all the nasty details of the trial here. But it is worth remembering that Carruth fled Charlotte once Adams died and was captured in Tennessee hiding in the trunk of a Toyota Camry. A female friend of Carruth's had driven the wide receiver to Tennessee in an effort to escape jail. Carruth's own mother told police where to find him.

That moment—when the Camry's trunk popped open and one of the Panthers' best hopes for the future rubbed his eyes, shoved aside a couple of water bottles filled with his own urine and crawled out of the trunk—served as the tragic signature moment of this team for several years.

I can't shed much light on Carruth's character, because he often boycotted the press for months at a time. No one was quite sure why. He was always a bit of a weird guy in the locker room, although I didn't consider him dangerous at the time.

I can tell you that after sitting through much of his trial, however, I certainly agreed with the jury's decision.

The longest conversation I ever had with Carruth involved, of all things, jersey numbers. This was about two months before the murder of Cherica Adams.

Carruth was obsessed about what number to wear. In only three seasons with the Panthers, he wore five numbers—86, 83, 18, 84 and 89.

Carruth liked 18 best, but at the time the NFL required almost all receivers to wear numbers in the 80s. Carruth played one game with No. 18, had a 100-yard game and then had a dream that night in which the Panthers' excellent equipment man, Jackie Miles, came to him and said the NFL was making him switch back to a number in the 80s.

The next day, Carruth told me, that's exactly what happened.

Carruth had worn No. 21 in college at Colorado and had decided he only looked good when his jersey included a "1."

"It makes me look slim," Carruth said. "I think I look fat in my uniform when I wear two block numbers."

Weird, huh?

Misfire

Even during some of their worst times, like the 4-12 season of 1998 in which Kerry Collins was released and Dom Capers fired, the Panthers could sometimes make their opponents mad.

Carolina fullback William Floyd made Tampa Bay linebacker Hardy Nickerson so angry on October 18, 1998, that Nickerson tried to spit at Floyd.

He did get a little on Floyd, too.

But most of it landed on an official.

Wildebeests and Lions

W hen George Seifert entered his first training camp as the Panthers' coach in 1999, everyone wondered what to expect from the man who had won two Super Bowl rings as a head coach for the San Francisco 49ers.

Seifert proved to be interesting, although not very successful. He was distant from his players—he really didn't want to know about their personal lives. But he did provoke them with a number of interesting analogies, such as telling them out of the blue, "Don't be a wildebeest!" in the first few days of his first training camp in Spartanburg.

Seifert, once a zoology major at Utah, explained later to the players about what a wildebeest (a type of African antelope) does when confronted by a lion.

"The story he gave," Panthers safety Mike Minter said following that practice, "is when the wildebeest gets caught by a lion and the lion grabs his neck, the wildebeest kind of gives up and gets wide-eyed. So what coach Seifert was saying was, 'Guys, don't be that wildebeest. Don't give up. Don't walk around here wide-eyed.'"

Wifely Coaching

A lthough Seifert would preach aggressiveness with the wildebeest analogy, he didn't always practice it.

One of his most timid calls came in September 1999, when the Panthers were leading Jacksonville, 14-6, and poised to put more points on the scoreboard. With the ball at their own 43, Carolina had 44 seconds left and some momentum. The Panthers needed about 20-25 yards to get in John Kasay's field-goal range.

Seifert, however, called one running play for two yards and let the clock go to 0:00. Those three extra points he might have gotten proved crucial—Carolina lost the game by two, 22-20.

"I can deal with listening to the radio and hearing that was a mistake," Seifert said. "I can deal with reading in the paper that was a mistake. But when my wife tells me that was a mistake, I'm in trouble."

Forget the Small Talk

Of the three Panthers' head coaches, Seifert was by far the worst at making small talk. He didn't care for it, didn't pretend to and generally acted in a one-on-one conversation like there was some other place he *really* needed to be.

Panthers play-by-play man Bill Rosinski has been a fixture on the Panthers' official radio and TV shows since the beginning. Coaches Dom Capers and John Fox both grew to trust Rosinski with inside information, knowing he wouldn't reveal it on air unless absolutely necessary.

But Rosinski couldn't pierce Seifert, either.

"When we did our TV show with George, we always taped him on Thursdays at 10:30 a.m.," Rosinski said. "Literally within a minute of 10:30, he'd walk in, say hello in a general way and sit down next to me. I'd try to chit chat. No chance. I'd say, 'How's everything going?' And he'd say, 'Good.' That was it. We'd tape three segments and when we were done, George would take the microphone off, walk out the door and say 'See ya.' We did it that way for 16 weeks."

Only once did Seifert ever bare his heart to Rosinski. That was when Bill Musgrave, then the offensive coordinator, abruptly quit Seifert's staff four games into the 2000 season. Musgrave had found Seifert difficult to work with.

"Seifert opened up to me that day after we talked about it a little bit about it on the pregame radio show," Rosinski said.

"When the interview was done, he usually just got out fast. But this time he just looked at me and said, 'The thing with Bill— that was like having your son tell you he didn't want to be in the family anymore.' And then he turned around and left."

Buckner and Seifert

B rentson Buckner joined the Panthers before the 2001 season as an unrestricted free agent and became a defensive line anchor on the Super Bowl squad of 2003. But he says if his visit to the Panthers had been structured a little differently, he would never have come to Carolina.

"I tell people all the time that if I had met George Seifert before I signed my deal rather than after, I never would have signed it," Buckner said. "I met a lot of the defensive coaches before I signed and Mr. Richardson, too. Then I signed and then I met George. You could tell right away how distant he was. There was no 'How is your family doing? Are you married?' None of that. He wouldn't really even look you in the eye that much when he talked to you. No personality. I walked out of that meeting, called my agent and said, 'If I had to do it all over again, I wouldn't sign here.'"

Greene and Steele

O ne of the darkest on-field afternoons in Panthers history came on December 13, 1998, when Panthers linebacker Kevin Greene suddenly grabbed his linebackers coach, Kevin Steele, near the neck and started forcibly shoving him backward during the middle of a game. Steele had been in Greene's face, talking heatedly to him, when Greene suddenly decided to get physical.

"I happened to have my head down and was staring at the sidelines," said Bill Rosinski, the radio voice of the Carolina Panthers. "All of a sudden I see Kevin Greene jump up and start choking Kevin Steele. The thing I remember most about it is this. You know how when in boxing a guy throws a punch and misses? But you know that, man, if he had landed that… That's what it sounded like. The reaction from the fans was like, 'Oooooohhh!'"

Dom Capers then made one of the worst decisions of his coaching career. After talking to both Greene and Steele on the sideline, he let Greene return to the game.

Capers would later suspend Greene for one game for the incident, and Greene would apologize to Steele and Panther fans for what he did.

"I lost my composure," Greene said. "What I did was wrong."

But Capers's decision to let Greene return to the game after such an obvious breach of coach-player conduct was one of the last bad decisions he would make—he got fired a couple of weeks later.

How to Lose Games Creatively, Part 1

In 1997, the Panthers were playing well in Minneapolis. Tied with Minnesota, 7-7 in the fourth quarter, Carolina was trying to make a goal-line stand on third and goal from the 3.

Minnesota quarterback Brad Johnson dropped back, threw the ball and had it swatted by Panthers nose tackle Greg Kragen.

End of play, right? Wrong. The ball bounced back into Johnson's hands, and the quarterback carried it into the end zone for a touchdown. It was believed to be the first time in NFL history that a quarterback had thrown a pass to himself for a TD. In the official boxscore, it read: "Johnson 3 pass from Johnson."

Said Johnson: "It was a play that I think will go into the memory banks of Vikings fans for years to come."

Said Kragen, shaking his head afterward and remembering the 13-5 season of 1996: "Last year, that doesn't happen to us."

Said Dwight Stone: "I think we started to know that right then we had used up all our breaks. The ball wasn't going to bounce our way for awhile."

How to Lose Games Creatively, Part II

In 2002, John Fox's first season, the Carolina Panthers were absolutely dominating the Dallas Cowboys in Irving, Texas. Carolina led 13-0 with less than five minutes to go. A victory would have pushed the Panthers to 4-2 and quite possibly helped them make the playoffs in Fox's first year as opposed to his second.

But then safety Deon Grant badly misjudged a Quincy Carter pass. Grant cut in front of Joey Galloway, thinking he was about to make an interception, but instead deflected the ball directly to Galloway. The surprised receiver gratefully galloped 80 yards for a touchdown.

Suddenly confident, Dallas stopped Carolina and drove down the field. The Cowboys converted on two fourth-and-long plays, scored on yet another tipped ball and won, 14-13.

Said Cowboys running back Emmitt Smith after that game: "It showed God has a sense of humor."

Fox, who hardly ever criticizes his team in public, said right after the loss he was more "ashamed" of that defeat than any he had ever suffered.

Carolina would lose five more games in a row, falling to 3-8 before finally getting out of the tailspin.

How to Lose Games Creatively, Part III

I still find this stat amazing. In 1998, the Panthers offense turned the ball over 10 times at the other team's 1-yard line or inside the 1. Those turnovers cost Carolina a possible 70 points.

15 Straight Losses

When the Panthers are 100 years old, it's almost certain that one of their team records will still stand.

The Panthers will never lose 15 straight games in a season again.

In the NFL, with its hard salary cap and evenly matched talent, that's almost impossible to do. But Carolina managed it in 2001, winning the first game against Minnesota and then dropping 15 in a row.

Said defensive tackle Brentson Buckner: "I almost had to go see a psychiatrist after that one."

"It was awful," Panthers center Jeff Mitchell said. "Absolutely unbelievable. I hardly ever get fined for anything. But I was so frustrated that year I got fined all the time by the league—almost $18,000 altogether."

Said guard Kevin Donnalley: "You didn't want any knives or ropes or guns anywhere around the facility that year. It was brutal."

Peppers to the Rescue

About the only thing 1-15 did do for Carolina was get them the No. 2 pick in the 2002 NFL draft. New coach John

Fox used that choice to select North Carolina defensive end Julius Peppers.

The Panthers knew all the stories about Peppers's raw athleticism—how he could dunk a basketball and turn backflips and the like—but they hadn't seen it in person until July 2002. Then Peppers did something so phenomenal on one of the first days of training camp that the story spread like wildfire through Spartanburg.

It only took three seconds in a one-on-one drill between offensive and defensive linemen. Peppers was lined up against Chris Terry, Carolina's three-year starter at right tackle.

Paul Boudreau, then the Panthers offensive line coach, was entering his 16th year in the NFL and was shocked by it.

Peppers first faked Terry inside. It was such a convincing feint that Terry steamed that way, determined to smash into the rookie.

But Peppers was already gone. He had come to a total stop, changed direction and run past Terry on the outside. Although the players started the drill only one yard apart, Peppers was never touched.

Boudreau told me this later that day.

"I was in Detroit," he said. "And Barry Sanders was the only guy I ever saw who could stop and start like that. What Julius did to Chris on that play—it was just unbelievable. I can tell you right now that Carolina has never had anybody in the history of this franchise like this guy. He's 284 pounds, but the way he moves, he looks like he's about 240. He's going to be a special, special pass rusher."

Chapter 13

Forever Sam Mills

Sam Mills is the most beloved, respected Carolina Panther of all time.

Trying to find someone to say a bad word about Mills is like trying to find someone to trash Mother Teresa. Mills was the first player to have his own statue displayed in front of the Panthers' stadium. He was a hard-charging, explosive inside linebacker for Carolina from 1995-97, leading the defense that pushed the 1996 Panthers to the NFC Championship game.

After retiring at age 38, Mills took two or three months off and started getting bored. He wanted to get into coaching and the Panthers gave him a chance—first as a special assistant to linebackers coach Kevin Steele, then as a full-fledged assistant coach once Steele left for a head-coaching job at Baylor.

Mills has been there ever since. He has been through the Panthers' worst and best times.

He has also had some worst and best times of his own. At age 44, Mills was diagnosed with colon cancer in August 2003. The original diagnosis he was given said that he might have as little as three months to live—and no more than a year.

*Panthers linebacker Sam Mills was a smart, tough player known for his explosive hits. New York Giants linebacker Lawrence Taylor once said those hits had to be "better than sex." Here Mills exults after Carolina upset San Francisco at home in 1996. (Photo by Christopher A. Record/*The Charlotte Observer*)*

"The doctors told me, 'Let's just see if we can get you to 2004,'" Mills recounted in an exclusive interview for this book on March 31, 2004.

Mills made it well beyond New Year's Day 2004. He says now that was the most special January 1 of his life.

"When the New Year came in, it had a different meaning to me than 'Hey, the ball dropped in New York,'" Mills said. "It was like I had cleared a hurdle. I had made it."

A month later, after undergoing three days of chemotherapy early in the week and fighting through chemo-induced sickness nearly all week, Mills coached on the sidelines for the Panthers in the Super Bowl.

Mills is a father of four. His oldest son, Sam Mills III, works for the Panthers doing a variety of jobs in the equipment room and on the sideline. The elder Mills knows his future is uncertain. At press time for this book, Mills said he was "getting better" and that his cancer had been "contained." He acknowledged, however, that he looks no more than two weeks ahead at a time.

But Mills also said firmly that he harbors no bitterness about his cancer.

"The thing about the whole cancer deal is because of what I do and the notoriety that I have, it's one of those things you can't do privately," Mills said. "That's part of it. But also there's a part of me that tells me that's probably why I was chosen, too. If you could see the faces of the people also undergoing treatment that I get a chance to talk to and meet.... And it's not Sam Mills the football player talking to a cancer patient. It's Sam Mills the cancer patient, talking with another cancer patient."

When I interviewed Mills in March 2004, it was impossible to ignore the subject of cancer. Mills didn't want to—he truly wants people to be educated about the disease so they can better help each other. He kept returning to it on his own.

But we also talked about his playing career, his favorite moments with the Panthers and his ambition.

"I would love to be a head coach," Mills said. "That's my ultimate goal. Being a defensive coordinator would be the next step. I feel like I'm about ready to do that. But right now it's a little tough with the in-and-out, in-and-out of treatment. The thing that's most important to me right now, even more than being a coordinator, is staying put. Because all of my treatments are here. Coaching here allows me to keep the same doctors. Treatment is really more important to me right now than the actual coaching."

You can read about all facets of Mills's life in this chapter. It is organized so that stories about Mills's fight with cancer alternate with stories about Mills's football career.

The Ultimate Compliment

To understand how good Sam Mills was and how hard he could hit, you could cite dozens of statistics. Or note his five Pro Bowls. Or ponder how good you have to be to make the halls of fame for the Panthers, the New Orleans Saints and the states of Louisiana and New Jersey.

Or, if you prefer a shorter version, you could just listen to one of the best compliments ever paid to Mills, given by fellow linebacker Lawrence Taylor many years ago.

"Just once," L.T. said of Mills, "I'd like to get a hit like he does. It has to be better than sex."

When I asked Mills about that quote years later, he said: "L.T. may be the best linebacker ever to play. To hear a guy say that or even feel that way about some of your hits—that he even knows what your hits are like—it's very flattering."

But c'mon, Sam.

Is a great hit really better than sex?

"I don't know," Mills smiled. "I guess it depends on who you're having sex with."

The Diagnosis

Even as an assistant coach, Sam Mills has retained a player's mentality. He always used training camp in Spartanburg as a chance to keep himself in shape. You would frequently see him jogging around the Wofford campus or sweating in the weight room between meetings.

But in the summer of 2003, all that was different. He felt listless and spent.

For five straight days, Mills couldn't make himself work out. He was dead tired. On the sixth day, he tried to work out but had so little energy he had to quit halfway through.

Something was wrong. Mills' urine had begun changing to a darker color. He itched incessantly.

Mills went to see the team trainer and then to a doctor. He wasn't at all concerned about cancer—he had had a colonoscopy only three months before and a full physical exam.

"But they start checking me," Mills said. "They do an ultrasound. They find lesions in my liver. A mass in my stomach. The doctor takes me into his office and says what they see is cancer—colon cancer."

Mills was shocked. "Cancer, doc? How could it be cancer? I just had a colonoscopy."

The doctor tried to be gentle, telling Mills the cancer was high enough up in his body that the colonoscopy must not have been able to detect it.

Mills still remembers the rest of the conversation vividly. "I said, 'What do we do next?' And the doctor said, 'I don't know what we can do, if we can treat it.' All this stuff is hitting me at once. I say, 'How long do I have to live?'"

The doctor's reply was startling.

Maybe three months. Maybe four months.

No more than a year.

Mills wanted to talk. To ask questions. To understand. But he only got out three more words: "Are you serious?"

And then he burst out crying.

Coming to Carolina

Sam Mills started awfully late to become a legend with the Panthers. He didn't even join the team until age 35, and played his first actual game with the Panthers at 36 on the 1995 expansion team.

But Mills had been impressed with the way Carolina had courted him as a free agent. The Panthers eagerly offered him a $2.8-million, two-year contract in 1995, their expansion season, because coach Dom Capers and defensive coordinator Vic Fangio were both anxious to get him.

New Orleans then matched the offer, but Mills felt it was a move the Saints made somewhat begrudgingly.

"After all that I'd done playing in New Orleans, it kind of bothered me that they were only going to pay me the money because they had to pay it and not because they wanted to pay it," Mills said. "To me, it's almost like inviting somebody to your party or to some special event because your mom says you've got to invite them. If I found out I was invited to an event because somebody forced you to invite me, I'd rather not be invited at all."

The Itching

It was only later, after the diagnosis, that Sam Mills remembered an ironic conversation he and Mark Fields had engaged in a few weeks before in July 2003.

At the beginning of training camp, neither Fields nor Mills knew they had cancer.

But they both knew they couldn't stop scratching themselves.

"I walked into the locker room one time and Mark has powder all over his body," Mills remembered. "He's getting dressed for practice. I say, 'What in the world have you got there?'"

"I can't stop itching, coach," Fields said.

"Me, too!" Mills said. "It must be something out on the field! They must be using some kind of chemicals out there."

Fields offered Mills some of the powder, but Mills declined.

At night, though, Mills would sometimes start itching so badly in Spartanburg that he had to take another shower.

Chronic itching is not always a sign of cancer, of course. But in this case, for both Fields and Mills, it was.

"Me and Mark laugh about it now," Mills said. "We ask each other if you need any powder."

Leather Helmets

Sam Mills didn't begin his NFL career until age 27. Undrafted out of Division III Montclair (N.J.) State, he was the first of Sam and Juanita Mills's 11 children to get a college degree. In his family's eyes, that made him a major success already.

But Mills's football career looked iffy after college. He got cut by both an NFL and CFL team before obtaining a high school teaching job in New Jersey, teaching students woodworking and photography for $13,600 a year.

Mills eventually latched on to a linebacker position in the USFL, signing a contract for $25,000 in an old Chevrolet conversion van. He became a USFL star and used that as a springboard to the NFL's New Orleans Saints. He then played nine seasons in New Orleans before coming to Carolina.

By the time the 5-9 Mills actually played a game for Carolina, he was 36. His teammates realized quickly that Mills enjoyed the give and take of locker room razzing—Mills would sometimes refer to himself as a player who was "short, balding and can't see very well."

So his teammates started making him the target of every "old" joke they could think of.

Said Willie Green, a receiver on the first Panthers teams: "Sam was like a father—no, a grandfather—to all of us. He was an icon even while he was still playing. We used to joke with him all the time, asking him how to play with leather helmets and no facemasks, or how it was to tackle Jim Brown, or what it felt like when TVs were only in black and white."

Green, like his teammates, loved to tease Mills because they loved him.

"Sam used to knock the heck out of people and then he'd help them up," Green said. "If he isn't in the Pro Football Hall of Fame (Mills isn't so far), there should be no hall of fame."

Fox Gets the Word

When coach John Fox was told one of his assistants had cancer, he had a split-second to think about who it was before the news was relayed. Fox thought of several older coaches on his staff and figured it must be one of them.

When he heard the name "Sam Mills," like everyone else, he was shocked. And when he heard the "three months-to-a-year-left-to-live" diagnosis, it hurt him to the bone.

"I knew this was going to affect our football team," Fox said. "I knew what Sam meant to the team, the coaching staff and the whole organization. I mean, the guy has a statue out front! I knew what it did to me, so I knew what it did to them."

Fox decided to keep the exact nature of the diagnosis from his players.

"You just can't present it that way, and I couldn't say those words anyway," Fox said. But the players understood from Fox's body language that Mills's colon cancer was far more serious than Mark Fields's Hodgkins disease.

Fox said the Panthers were affected on the field by Mills's diagnosis in their final preseason game of 2003.

"We played like crap against Pittsburgh because of that," Fox said. "When I showed the film, I said this is what it looks like when we're not mentally into what we are doing. We were able to build on that. The best thing we could do for Sam, I told them, was to win games."

Learning From Foxy

Sam Mills has worked under all three of the Panthers' head coaches—Dom Capers, George Seifert and Fox. He has liked all of them, and he feels comfortable with Fox's coaching style because it is similar to his own.

"Foxy's memory and his recall are so fast," Mills said. "He can do a lot of things at once. I haven't seen anybody quite like Foxy who can look at stuff, see where this guy is, where that guy is, who knows the down and distance, who knows what they're signaling in and what we're signaling in. You just go, 'Man, does this guy ever stop?'"

Continued Mills: "One of the things about Foxy that makes him a good coach is he always tells those guys he's just an older version of them. And he acts like that. You don't always need to be in a player's face talking to them about football. He could be talking to them about their music. About their clothing. About their kids. About hobbies. About tattoos if they have one.

"When I was a player, if a coach was in the locker room, I really didn't want him in there coaching me up all the time. Just because you see me doesn't mean you have to give me more instruction. Foxy does a real good job of that. And I try to do it, too. Just chat to them about whatever. 'What are you listening to on that headset?' That sort of thing."

Richardson's Role

Panthers owner Jerry Richardson had been directly touched by cancer himself. In 1996, he had been diagnosed with prostate cancer and had successful surgery. His first-born son, Jon, also has battled cancer.

Richardson learned about Sam Mills's cancer immediately. After the diagnosis, Mills and one of his doctors drove to Richardson's house that night.

Mills's family was in New Jersey at the time, where they also keep a house. Richardson told Mills: "Look, you're not going to be alone. Either you stay here with me or I'll come down and stay with you."

"You've got the nicer house," Mills smiled. "I'll stay with you."

For the next few days, Jerry Richardson and his wife Rosalind took care of Mills. And the Panthers' owner stayed with Mills in the hospital.

"When I go to the hospital for more tests a day or two later, he's right there," Mills said. "He's carrying my bag in. I wake up from the anesthesia, he's sitting over there in the corner. He's answering my telephone. Folding my clothes up. Telling me to rest. He wanted to make sure I got the best care."

The Shovel Pass

Sam Mills keyed the Panthers' first ever victory, in 1995, with one of the most famous plays in team history.

Carolina was playing the New York Jets in Clemson. It was a home game for Carolina—the Panthers' new stadium wasn't ready yet. Carolina was 0-5 and there had been speculation that the team could become the first NFL squad to end up 0-16.

But Mills changed that. Very late in the first half and Carolina trailing, 12-6, Mills intercepted a shovel pass from Jets quarterback Bubby Brister and returned it 36 yards for a touchdown, sparking Carolina's 26-15 win.

On the play, Mills remembers now, the Panthers had a blitz called. New York Jets guard Roger Duffy was supposed to stay in place if there was a blitz, but instead he pulled. Mills blitzed untouched through the opening, ending up in the Jets' backfield within a second of the ball being snapped.

"The way it happened, it just kind of clicked," Mills said. "Right call, right place, right time. I intersected with where the Jets' back, Adrian Murrell, was supposed to be. I was never touched at all. I know I surprised Brister."

Brister, in mid-pitch, couldn't stop himself from throwing the ball. Mills gratefully accepted it and starting chugging the other way.

"The players today always tease me about that run," Mills said. "They say, 'Man, you were running slow.' But I say, 'Hey, I got there.'"

At the time, his teammates teased him, too. Said Panthers quarterback Frank Reich, noting there were only 22 seconds left before half when the play began: "I thought he was trying to do two things—score a TD and run out the clock."

Years later, Brister would tell Charles Chandler of *The Charlotte Observer* that the play dealt a serious blow to his career and helped create a negative image of him that kept him out of the NFL entirely for the 1996 season.

"I was scarred by it," Brister said. "I got beat up about it over and over again."

That was one of the biggest plays for Mills of the season, but it was far from his only one. Although 1995 didn't conclude with one of Mills's five trips to the Pro Bowl as a player, he now believes it was the best season of his career.

Mills ended that season with career highs in interceptions (five), sacks (4.5), forced fumbles (six) and fumble recoveries (four).

"I made a lot of big plays that season," Mills said. "I had this attitude that you've got to take chances because of the type of team we had. So I took a lot more than I usually did."

The Treatment

Ever since Sam Mills's cancer diagnosis, he has undergone the same treatment routine. Every two weeks he spends three days getting chemotherapy in Charlotte. The first two days are spent in an "infusion center" in Charlotte, where he undergoes chemotherapy along with other cancer patients. Liquid drugs are pumped into a port in his chest for about seven hours on Monday and Tuesday and then another several hours on Wednesday at his home.

"For those three chemo days, it's almost like you go into hibernation," Mills said.

When Mills enters the infusion center these days, it's like he's "Norm" from the old *Cheers* TV comedy.

"Sa-a-a-a-am!" the people shout. It was especially nice for Mills on Mondays after the Panthers won a game in the fall.

"You should see the smiles, the joy on those people's faces when we win," Mills said. "Here's an older person with a bag of chemicals, they're just smiling away because we won that game. Those things, man, they make you feel so good."

Mills has a way that he explains chemotherapy to people who have never had it.

"It's like if no one had ever developed a weed killer and you put something down in your yard to kill the good grass, the weeds, everything," Mills said. "And you're just going to start all over. It kills good cells, bad cells—everything. That's why you've got to rebuild yourself."

Mills was lucky. His body was not as adversely affected by chemotherapy as many are. Until the week of the Super Bowl, his treatments never made him throw up. He didn't have to worry about losing his hair, because he had already shaved off the little he had anyway. His black skin did turn a few shades lighter, he said, but that was difficult to notice unless you were around him all the time.

The infusion center tries to make its patients as comfortable as possible. They sit in easy chairs and can watch their own

At the Super Bowl in early 2004, Mills was just glad to be alive. Originally, doctors said cancer might kill him before the end of 2003. Here Mills speaks to the media four days before the Super Bowl. (Photo by Patrick Schneider/The Charlotte Observer)

personal TV. Mills usually brought his laptop computer, fresh from a download by the Panthers of game film on Carolina's next opponent.

But the treatments have been no picnic for him.

"When those treatment days are over, your body and your mind are both tired," Mills said. "I don't want to hear the radio. I don't want to see a TV. I don't even want to see the light. I turn the lights off in the house. It's like all of your senses are tired—your eyes, your ears, everything."

Mills said in our interview in March 2004 that the treatments have been helping him. He looked fit, still at his 225-pound playing weight.

"I do know I'm getting better," Mills said, "and thank God for that. My body has been able to tolerate the medication, although it does get tougher the longer you go. I get tingling sensations in my fingers and toes a lot. But that's something I've just learned to live with and keep going."

Mills's Favorite Games

Sam Mills has basically been involved in every game the Panthers have ever played as either a player or a coach. Ask him to name his favorite three, and he doesn't hesitate.

"The first Dallas playoff game had to be one," Mills said, referring to Carolina's playoff win over the Cowboys in 1997. That game also marked Mills's first and only playoff win as a player. "That was a real big moment. We knocked off the big kids on the block at that time."

Mills's next favorite? The first Tampa Bay game of 2003, when Kris Jenkins blocked the kick to send the game into overtime and Carolina eventually won. "That game I felt like brought our team to light as far as perseverance, hanging in there, never giving up," Mills said. "I mean, to block an extra point against the world champions and to beat them on their home field? It said a lot about what we had to do and where we wanted to go."

No. 3?

"The third one would have to be the Philadelphia game in the NFC Championship in Philly," Mills said, referring to Carolina's 14-3 win on January 18, 2004. "To see us finally do it. To know that when the game is over, our next stop is the Super Bowl. That was so special to me."

Sierra

Sam Mills's children have quite a spread in age. As of early 2004, Mills had a 25-year-old son, Sam III, who also worked for the Panthers. He also had two 20-year-old children, Marcus and Larissa. And he and his wife, Melanie, had a six-year-old daughter, Sierra.

Mills tried to spend as much time with his daughter as he could. And he told her about his cancer in simple terms, figuring someone else would if he didn't.

Once, after the diagnosis, the two of them had to park far away from the entrance in a crowded parking lot at the monstrous Concord Mills outlet mall near Charlotte.

"Why'd we park so far away?" Sierra asked her dad.

"We need the exercise," Sam said.

"Do I look like I need exercise?" Sierra asked.

"Oh no, baby," Sam said. "It's just that exercise is good for you."

"Daddy," Sierra said, "you always told me you work out so you can live a long time and be around for me."

"That's true," Sam said, wondering where this one was headed.

"Well, how come they're saying you won't live a long time now?" Sierra persisted.

Sam smiled.

"Oh, baby," Sam said softly. "Dad's going to be around."

Chapter 14

Weird Stuff

Through the years, the Carolina Panthers have made for some downright bizarre headlines.

Bill Rosinski, the only radio play-by-play voice the Panthers have ever had, explains it well.

"I was the voice of the Atlanta Falcons for three years before I came to Charlotte, and I thought by then I had seen it all," Rosinski says. "Deion Sanders was helicoptering back and forth between the Atlanta Braves and the Falcons. Andre Rison was dating Lisa 'Left Eye' Lopes, the rap star, and she burned his house down. Jerry Glanville was the coach, and he was a constant trip in himself. But then I come to this team, and all of that turns out to be Tiddlywinks."

Not only have the Panthers produced a constant stream of stories over the years, but so have their fans. This chapter chronicles some of those as well, because what is a team without its supporters?

Read on for stories about the Panther who became a reality TV star, the Panther who wears fur coats and some of the Carolina fans who will do absolutely anything not to miss a game.

The Bloody Claw

If you've ever seen Panthers' offensive tackle Jordan Gross, you know that his last name doesn't describe him accurately at all. Gross is one of the nicest, most baby-faced guys in the NFL. He only had to shave three times a week when he first entered the league.

"Jordan is basically like everyone's little brother," center Jeff Mitchell said.

But Gross had something very gross happen to him once at a restaurant, and so many of his teammates were around he will never quite live it down.

Gross was the Panthers' first-round draft pick of 2003 and Bruce Nelson, another offensive lineman, was the second-round choice. The veteran offensive linemen heard that and started salivating.

Rookies typically have to buy veterans at least a few meals during the season, and early-round draft choices are always opening their wallets.

On this particular night, Nelson was treating everyone to dinner and most of the offensive line had shown up. They were deep into the appetizers when Gross let out a primal scream of pain.

"What happened?" Kevin Donnalley asked.

"Something jabbed into my tongue," Gross said.

"Oh, shut up, rookie," Mitchell said jokingly. "Don't be a wuss. You just bit your tongue."

Gross said it was more than that, though. And he was right. He was bleeding. He had just suffered an unintentional tongue piercing.

Said Donnalley: "Turns out he's got this *thing* about an inch long in his tongue. We're trying to pull it out, but we can't. It almost looked like a part of a claw from a lobster or crab that got in the batter by accident. And it's got these barbs on it that won't let it come out."

Mitchell had a pocketknife with some scissors on one of the blades. So he got that out and they tried to use those to extract it. Thankfully, no further damage was done with that bright idea.

Fortunately for Gross, by strange coincidence one of the Panthers' team doctors was actually at the same restaurant, eating in the next room with a different group. The offensive linemen found the doctor and he took Gross with him, back to his office, to extract the piece of claw.

All ended well.

Both Gross and the doctor returned to dinner before long. But by then, Gross's appetizer was gone.

While everyone else had stopped eating, too grossed out to continue, Mitchell had cheerfully finished it off.

"Hey, he wasn't going to eat it!" Mitchell said.

A Guaranteed Butt-Kicking

No single fan has ever had a more obvious effect on a football game than Joe Muscarello, a Panther supporter who bills himself as the "Carolina Prowler."

Muscarello wears a furry black outfit to home games, with huge black paws and a miniature panther perched on each shoulder like a parrot. He's well known enough that his picture has been in the Pro Football Hall of Fame as part of an exhibit about NFL fans.

For the November 9, 2003, home game against Tampa Bay—an emotion-filled contest that included a bunch of trash-talking on both sides of the field—the Panthers selected Muscarello as "Fan of the Game." Typically, the selection is shown live on the big screen in the stadium during a break, and the fan says "Thank you" or "Go Panthers," and that's that.

Not this time.

Muscarello, like many other fans in the stadium, had read in the newspaper about Tampa Bay defensive end Simeon Rice "guaranteeing" a win over Carolina.

So he grabbed the offered microphone early in the fourth quarter and, with Carolina leading, yelled: "Let me tell you something, Warren Sapp and Simeon Rice. You *guaranteed* a win. We *guarantee* we're going to kick your butt."

The other fans roared in delight when Muscarello trash-talked the Buccaneers. But the taunt fired up the Bucs defense. Both Sapp and Rice gleefully pointed to the scoreboard, where Muscarello's picture had just been shown, and then Rice quick-ly sacked Jake Delhomme twice. It was as if the taunts had given the Bucs an extra shot of adrenaline just when they were about to falter.

Said Panthers defensive tackle Brentson Buckner of the fan's comments: "It was good that he thought that, but he need-ed to say it with 30 seconds on the clock when we're up by 10!"

Before long, Carolina had fallen behind, 24-20, as Tampa Bay scored 17 consecutive fourth-quarter points. And the Carolina Prowler (a banking loan specialist during the week) had left his seat. Although he hadn't been threatened, he still feared for his own safety and that of his nine-year-old son if the Panthers lost.

Delhomme and the offense saved the day with a last-minute touchdown drive, however. And then everyone had fun with Muscarello's taunt.

"I don't know who he is, but my God!" Delhomme said. "We have racehorses back home. Maybe I can order a muzzle."

Joked Panthers center Jeff Mitchell: "That guy, we need to seek him out and revoke his season ticket privileges."

Buckner stuck up for the fan. "That's what you want from your fans, really," Buckner said. "You put a mike in front of somebody in the stands and ask that question in Philly or Tampa or Pittsburgh, and you'd get the same reaction."

Muscarello felt bad about the whole thing, knowing he had escaped by a hair becoming the Panthers' answer to notori-

*Emotions ran high at the Tampa Bay/Carolina game on November 9, 2003. They ran so high, in fact, that the Panthers fan who bills himself as the "Carolina Prowler" taunted Warren Sapp and Simeon Rice over the loudspeakers, almost contributing to a Carolina loss. (Photo by Patrick Schneider/*The Charlotte Observer*)*

ous Chicago Cubs fan Steve Bartman. So a few days later, Muscarello came by a Panthers practice to apologize to coach John Fox.

"Don't sweat that," Fox told the fan. "You were fired up. I like people who get fired up. We just need to keep you off the big screen."

The Panthers continued the "Fan of the Game" promotion, but were careful not to relinquish control of the microphone for the rest of the season.

A Sacrifice to Football Gods

One of my all-time favorite Panther fans is Beverly Knight. She was my English teacher my senior year at Dorman High School in Spartanburg, S.C. Somehow I spent nine months in her wonderfully challenging class without realizing the depth of her football passion.

Knight spent the first seven years of her life in northern Alabama, and by then she was already imprinted with a love of football. One of Bear Bryant's houndstooth hats hung on a peg in her grandmother's living room, right beside a picture of Jesus.

"There is nothing more wonderful than the feeling that comes with winning, and nothing more horrible than the aftermath of a loss," Knight said.

Knight eventually ended up in Spartanburg, where she taught English for 28 years. Part of a group that owns four PSLs, Knight has missed exactly one home game in nine seasons. She also attends about 25 training-camp practices each year in Spartanburg. Her all-time favorite Panthers: Willie Green and Will Witherspoon.

Knight almost missed the Panthers' first ever win, on October 15, 1995. She was caught up in a six-car pileup on the way to the game, but unhurt. Rather than stay with her car, she got in a friend's van and continued to Clemson.

"I left the car on the side of the road, with instructions to the tow-truck driver to let my insurance company know where he towed it," Knight said. "Because I had the son of a good friend with me, and he was distraught that my new car had been crushed, I consoled him by telling him that we had sacrificed the beautiful green Thunderbird to the gods of football. If they accepted our sacrifice, they'd reward us with a win."

Consider the sacrifice accepted. Thanks in part to Sam Mills's interception return of a shovel pass, Carolina won the game, 26-15.

Another Near-Miss

The first Panthers fan to nearly miss a Carolina game through no fault of his own has to be Leonard Burch, who owns the Superior Mechanical company in Charlotte.

Burch and a friend had decided to go to Carolina's first ever game—a 1995 exhibition against Jacksonville in the annual Hall of Fame preseason contest at Canton, Ohio.

The two were going with a Broach Sports Tour group and had planned to meet at Burch's shop first. But Burch's friend, James Warren, overslept. The duo was in even worse shape time-wise than they thought, because they were holding an outdated itinerary. Just as they were about to pull off the highway to meet the tour buses, they saw the Broach buses pulling onto the highway.

Unsure whether there were more buses to come, Burch and Warren waited awhile and then got panicky. They called Tom Broach, the tour's unflappable leader, on his cellular phone. Broach told them the bus couldn't stop, but they could probably catch up to it because it would make several stops along the way.

Because Warren's car was ancient, the two rented a car in Statesville and sped up Interstate 77 toward Charleston, West Virginia, where the tour group was supposed to stop and eat lunch.

"I don't think we ever got below 80," Burch said of the 225-mile drive.

They found the buses in a mall parking lot in Charleston and actually got there a few minutes before they were to leave. The bus driver told them to go ahead and grab a quick lunch now that they were here, they had time.

When the two came out of Chick-Fil-A, however, with their "to-go" lunches, they saw the buses moving one more time.

"We got panicky again," Burch said. "I threw my lunch in the trash before I ate a single bite, and we both ran toward the buses as fast as we could."

One bus stopped.

The same driver opened the door, his face red with laughter.

"We're not leaving!" the driver said. "We're just circling around to the front of the mall to pick everyone else up."

Burch and Warren finally made it onto the bus. They left their rent-a-car in the West Virginia mall's parking lot and picked it up on the way home. Their desperate attempt to make the Panthers' first game become enough of a Panthers fan legend that even Jerry Richardson heard about it and will tell the story occasionally.

A Wild Plane Ride

I've been on a lot of planes filled with Panther fans going to games over the years, but never one any wilder than the one I rode on January 10, 2004. That was the morning of the Panthers-St. Louis playoff game.

It was a small, 60-seat plane, and completely full. Panther fans in full regalia filled about 50 of those seats. The lone flight attendant got into the spirit of things, holding a couple of impromptu contests.

At one point, a man threw a Panther football over his head, and the person who caught the football was given a free beer.

Believe me, by that point he didn't really need it.

Catching a Sauerbrun Punt

One of my favorite experiences in all my years of covering the Panthers was the time I convinced Todd Sauerbrun

Panther fans have long had a unique bond with their team. Here wide receiver Steve Smith climbs high for a little love during the Panthers' win over Detroit in December 2003. (Photo by Christopher A. Record/The Charlotte Observer)

during the summer of 2003 to go out onto a high school football field in Charlotte and kick punts to me for a story that was published in *The Charlotte Observer.*

I never understood why Steve Smith would sometimes spin the ball triumphantly after making, say, a fair catch at the 10-yard line. What was the big deal about that? After seeing Sauerbrun's punts plummet down from the sky, I understood.

There's nothing easy about catching a punt—and of course I was doing it without 10 men bearing down on me intent on decapitation.

Sauerbrun has the mindset of a strong safety, but he plays punter because he's so good at it. He hates not getting onto the field more. He once got a 15-yard unsportsmanlike conduct penalty during a game for taunting an opposing punt returner after knocking him down on a tackle. He broke his nose on a tackle once for the Panthers and stayed in the game. He sometimes tames his competitive instinct in the off season by playing professional-caliber racquetball.

He can give you his punting philosophy in five words: "Just whack the ball, brother."

When those punts were bearing down on me that afternoon, I was worried.

About my teeth. About my health. About everything.

Sauerbrun was happily quoting lines from the Will Ferrell movie *Old School*—he has seen it dozens of times—but I didn't feel like laughing.

As Philadelphia kicker David Akers once said of Sauerbrun: "Watching him punt is like watching a football being shot out of a cannon."

I managed to catch a few of the punts. It turned out that the toughest ones weren't the booming 70-yarders that turned over and spiraled nicely. The toughest ones to catch were the mishits—the 45-yarders that turned crazily in the sky.

I asked Sauerbrun after the session how it felt when he hit one just right, like the 85-yarder that had blasted over my head.

"I just describe it like this," Sauerbrun said. "It tastes so good."

More Than 10 Seconds of Fame

Only the most diehard Carolina Panther fans remember Ryan Sutter, whose NFL career ended 10 seconds after it began.

Sutter got into one game for Carolina, in 1998. As a rookie safety, he tried to make a tackle on the first play of his first NFL game and dislocated his shoulder.

But all ended well for Sutter, who may have gotten more prime-time TV exposure than any Panther ever. He ended up being the pick of *The Bachelorette*—Trista Rehn—in a wildly popular TV show. Their ensuing marriage was chronicled breathlessly in various tabloid and entertainment shows. (Jake Delhomme and his wife, Keri, are fans of both *The Bachelor* and *The Bachelorette*, incidentally).

Sutter always had a good sense of humor in the Panther locker room, although he wasn't nearly as mushy there as he appeared to be in *The Bachelorette*. Once, on a conference call after the show made him famous, Sutter told reporters that, contrary to rumor, Trista wasn't pregnant.

"But," Sutter said proudly, "I am."

Dressed to Impress

R od "He Hate Me" Smart is widely known as one of the most eccentric players the Panthers had. It's not just the nickname. It's not just the way he once stood up in the middle of a team meeting to give coach John Fox a big hug. It's also the way he wore vintage clothing on game days—stuff that he had often bought at local thrift shops.

"Rod saved his best clothing for game days," Kevin Donnalley said. "The shock of that first walk-in was what he lived for, I think, not the winning of the game. When he walked in with leopard print, platform heels, a fur hat, a fur jacket and a disco outfit that first look from everybody—everybody screaming and laughing—that's what he lived for. He would be pimped out and proud of it."

Said Mike Rucker: "As far as eccentric goes, Jarrod Cooper may give Rod Smart a run for the money. But I'd have to say that Rod probably edges him out."

The Chicken Run

It has been a long tradition for the Panthers for rookies to have to bring chicken to the team plane on away trips.

It works like this. The team plane usually leaves Saturday afternoon for Sunday road games. Everyone meets at the stadium before that and then buses over to the airport.

The chicken of choice? Usually fried. Usually Bojangles' (a chicken-and-biscuit chain based in Charlotte) or KFC.

Said Mike Rucker: "I remember being real stressed out as a rookie, having to be at the stadium at a certain time and still having to get the chicken. You'd be waiting in line, looking at your watch, knowing you didn't have much time. And you had to bring it. If you didn't, the guys were going to jump all over you."

In 2003, Ricky Manning was one of the chicken guys. Even after the cornerback made three interceptions in the NFC Championship game, Manning still had his duties.

"I'm still a rookie, don't forget it," Manning said during Super Bowl week. "I still have to help feed the other DBs two or three times a week. We get them Buffalo wings during the week. And then it's always Bojangles' chicken Saturday afternoons on the plane."

The Sunday Doubleheader

One of the weirdest games the Panthers ever played was also the first time Jake Delhomme ever took the field in Charlotte.

No, it wasn't Carolina vs. Jacksonville in 2003. It was Carolina against New Orleans on January 2, 2000, and Delhomme was playing for the other team.

Carolina, entering the game at 7-8, had to win by as big a margin as possible and hope for a lot of help to make the play-offs. The Panthers trailed Green Bay by 18 points in the key tiebreaker differential, meaning that if both teams won, Green Bay's victory would have to be by at least 18 fewer points than Carolina. Some other stuff would have to happen, too, but that was No.1.

So the Panthers, led by quarterback Steve Beuerlein and his five touchdown passes, did all sorts of wild stuff. Leading 45-7 with 1:41 remaining, Carolina went for it on fourth and 10 from their own 39 (and missed).

Delhomme didn't exactly have a field day against Carolina as New Orleans starter that day. It was one of just two games he started in six seasons as a Saint. He threw four interceptions and only one touchdown. But Delhomme did sneak in for a touch-down with 18 seconds left in the game, closing the door on any hope of a Panther playoff berth. The way Delhomme never quit in the game, even when his team was down by 38 points, impressed Panthers general manager Marty Hurney.

It would be three years later that Delhomme would take the field in Charlotte again, this time in a Panthers jersey against Jacksonville in September 2003.

And then, finally, the Panthers' fortunes would start to change.

Afterword

Jake Delhomme remembers the rope.

At the Super Bowl, as soon as the game is over, NFL security people stretch ropes all the way around the field.

The winning team stays inside the long rectangle formed by the ropes, which becomes a VIP section. The losers are herded to the outside and urged to head toward the exits. It's the NFL's none-too-subtle way of getting the losing team off the field so the celebration can begin.

Most of the Carolina Panthers were more than happy to get away from the scene of their heartbreaking 32-29 Super Bowl loss to New England. They got to their locker room in Houston's Reliant Stadium quickly.

But the Panthers quarterback stayed on the field for several minutes, watching the Patriots hoist the Vince Lombardi Trophy and hug each other.

Delhomme would later call these moments "tasting the pain."

"It's just the worst feeling in the world," Delhomme said afterward. "You can't explain it."

But Delhomme had a good reason for making himself feel bad. He wanted to burn the memory into his brain for the 2004 season and beyond with the Panthers.

"I just wanted to watch the celebration and let it hurt even more," Delhomme said. "When there are two-a-days in the off-season, when a lot of us are going to be complaining and whining, then we have to keep working and try to get to the other side of that rope."

The euphoria of the Panthers' run to the Super Bowl had yet to wear off in Charlotte when I conducted most of the interviews for this book in the spring of 2004. As defensive end Mike Rucker said: "Coming back here, to be honest with you, you couldn't tell that you lost the Super Bowl. People keep coming up and saying, 'Hey, we're proud of you guys.' I don't think they're saying that in Philadelphia. That's what I love about the Carolinas."

The Panthers' franchise has been in a similar position to this once before, in 1996. After that fine sprint to the NFC Championship game, however, the team fell hard. From the players to team owner Jerry Richardson, everyone wrongly figured it would be easy to get back to the playoffs for many years in a row after that.

Instead, it took Carolina seven long years to even make the playoffs again.

How will the Panthers deal with success this time?

Said coach John Fox: "I'm not big on predictions. I like our football team. But we have some youth. And we have a good core."

The Panthers have finally gotten noticed on a national basis, at least. Carolina earned a scheduling plum for the 2004 opener, receiving a home *Monday Night Football* game against Green Bay.

The Panthers' karma of 2003 can never be exactly duplicated, of course, because NFL teams change their roster by about one-third every season. The Panthers lost a number of starters from the Super Bowl team in the first months of 2004.

Cornerback Reggie Howard and offensive guard Jeno James both signed for big money with the Miami Dolphins. Safety Deon Grant left for the same reason to Jacksonville. Offensive guard Kevin Donnalley retired. Offensive tackle Todd Steussie got cut—he wasn't a bad player, but his salary-cap figure was too high—and was quickly picked up by Tampa Bay.

By the end of 2003, though, I wouldn't have considered any of those players to have been among the top dozen Panther players—the nucleus of the team.

Carolina tried to add a number of mid-priced free agents in the spring of 2004, such as cornerback Artrell Hawkins, linebackers Jessie Armstead and Brandon Short and offensive tackle Adam Meadows. But the Panthers' biggest off-season acquisitions were likely made in the 2004 draft.

The Panthers got good again in 2003 in large part because they had nailed their top draft picks for three years in a row prior to that. First-round picks like Jordan Gross, Dan Morgan and Julius Peppers came through. Steve Smith (a third-rounder) and Kris Jenkins (a second-rounder) also emerged as possible NFL superstars.

In 2004, the Panthers took a gamble in the NFL draft's first round—Chris Gamble.

Gamble went to Ohio State as a wide receiver but switched to cornerback and then entered the NFL draft after his junior year. Everyone says Gamble is very raw, but the Panthers liked him so much they traded up from No.31 to No.28 to get him.

Carolina liked the fact that Gamble had been productive for Ohio State, which won a national championship in 2002 with Gamble starting both ways.

"He didn't play at Podunk University," Fox said. "He's been in some big spots. Playing on a national championship stage is big, particularly for a young guy."

Ideally, the Panthers would like Gamble to become an elite cornerback who could team with Ricky Manning as the club's starting cornerbacks for the rest of the decade. They also are intrigued by Gamble's wide-receiving and kick-returning skills and may eventually give him spot duty in both those places as well.

The Panthers also have tried to enhance Delhomme's weaponry in the offseason. They chose two wide receivers in the 2004 draft—second-round pick Keary Colbert of Southern Cal and fifth-rounder Drew Carter of Ohio State.

Colbert is a steady possession receiver who set a Southern Cal record for career pass receptions. Said Fox: "He's got outstanding quickness and is probably as good a route runner as anybody who came out in the draft."

Carter actually has more speed than Colbert, but he had two major knee injuries at Ohio State, and another at Carolina in an early minicamp and isn't expected to contribute much until the 2005 season. The Panthers also chose an interesting linebacker in the sixth round—Colorado's Sean Tufts. He sounds like he might give an extra edge to the special teams.

Said Tufts: "Flying down on kickoffs with your ears pinned back and your hair on fire—that's my game."

Carolina's other major addition in 2004 and beyond could be a familiar name—linebacker Mark Fields. I thought Fields was the Panthers' overall MVP in 2002. Then Fields missed the entire 2003 season with cancer.

Fields, though, could be a force if he returns at full strength. An enthusiastic soul, he will also help team morale if he comes back.

Of course, there is no guarantee that the Panthers will return to the Super Bowl within a year or two even if all of those players work out beautifully. The NFL is so evenly matched these days that it is extremely difficult to navigate through the playoffs. The Panthers lived on a knife blade for much of the 2003 season—that's part of the reason the year was so thrilling.

The Panthers will always have the memories of 2003 to sustain them, though, when times get tough again. Any team that can beat St. Louis and Philadelphia back to back in the playoffs—and on the road—can do just about anything.

So it will be great fun watching the Panthers in their second decade as a franchise and beyond. Because as the Panthers have proven beyond a shadow of a doubt during their first decade, you never exactly know when they are going to win or lose.

But you always know it's going to be entertaining.

Celebrate the Heroes of Professional Sports
in These Other Releases from Sports Publishing!

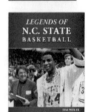

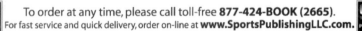